Complete Poems
1965–2020

Complete Poems
1965–2020

Michael Butterworth

ISBN 978-1-7328257-7-2

Text © Michael Butterworth
www.michael-butterworth.co.uk
Introduction © Jim Burns
Cover photo © 1968 Ted Johnson

Edited by Jean-Paul L. Garnier
Book design by F. J. Bergmann
Cover by Jean-Paul L. Garnier & Misen

First Hardcover Edition | 2023

Space Cowboy Books
61871 29 Palms Hwy.
Joshua Tree, CA 92252
www.spacecowboybooks.com

Dedications

Tony Stimson, who told me to reconcile the two sides of my nature – the part that identifies with the earth and the part that wanders away into space.

John H Clark, who graded my early attempts – and taught concision.

Jimmy Foster, who taught me to re-find my way by returning to the beginning.

By the Same Author

My Servant the Wind (a novel)
Butterworth (collected short fiction)
Complete Poems: 1965 – 2000
The Blue Monday Diaries: In the Studio with New Order
The Savoy Book (ed., with David Britton)
Savoy Dreams (ed., with David Britton)

WILD FLIGHTS

The Time of the Hawklords (with Michael Moorcock)

Queens of Deliria (Hawklords 2)

Ledge of Darkness (graphic novel, Hawklords 3
    with Bob Walker)

Space 1999: Planets of Peril
Space 1999: Mind-Breaks of Space (with J Jeff Jones)
Space 1999: The Space-Jackers
Space 1999: The Psychomorph
Space 1999: The Time Fighters
Space 1999: The Edge of the Infinite
Space 1999: Year Two Omnibus

AC/DC: Hell Ain't No Bad Place to Be (as Richard Bunton)

SIGNIFICANT AGENCY

Brion Gysin: Here to Go: Planet R101 (by Terry Wilson)
68 Cantos (prose-poems by William Weiss)

CO-AUTHOR

Lord Horror (by David Britton)
Return from the Wild (the story of Lassie the fox-dog,
    by John Roberts Warren)

EDITOR

All novels in the Lord Horror sequence by David Britton:
    Lord Horror
    Lord Horror: Reverbstorm
    Motherfuckers: The Auschwitz of Oz
    Baptised in the Blood of Millions
    La Squab: The Black Rose of Auschwitz
    Invictus Horror
    Razor King
    Old Death

Contents

Introduction

How to read this book? It has all the conventional trappings, including a list of publications where some of the poems first appeared. And yet I find it impossible to think of it as simply a collection of poems. That suggests individual items which can be singled out for commentary by pointing to their subject-matter, technical aspects, and intended impact. The seasoned critic of contemporary poetry can easily construct an introduction to such an assemblage of poems, selecting a few for a useful quotation or two and generalising about the rest.

Not so with Michael Butterworth's work. Its interest and its impact rest on the fact that it is, in effect, one long poem, built up over the years. Its continuity is essential to its existence. It has an overall cohesion that can only come from an acceptance of all its strengths and its weaknesses. Without it there would be a lack of substance that could easily lead to it losing the reader's attention. Not every portion of it is perfect, any more than the personality of the author can be perfect. And in many ways that may be the point of the poetry. It shows that it's the product of a flawed human being who, like the rest of us, has to come to terms with the fact that life makes its demands and we don't always respond in a satisfactory manner. To turn these responses into a basis for poetry requires honesty if the poet wants to avoid being merely self-justifying in what he writes.

Butterworth's way of working, as I perceive it, is to combine reflections on the real world that is all around us with excursions into what might be called the light fantastic. I was tempted to say the surreal, but it's now a hackneyed word too often used to describe anything that appears to wander away from the ordinary. But with Butterworth we are in a kind of parallel universe when his writing applies itself to what is behind his eyes rather than what is front of them. The mind turns inwards as well as outwards, and either way can make for a voyage of discovery. The constant flow of reactions, whether emanating from sights seen or reflection on them, keep the work firmly anchored in the poet's life and thoughts. It doesn't seem jarring when the writing switches in its intentions. The everyday can quickly slide into the strange.

A few words about the technique behind the poems might be appropriate. It could be claimed that it's mostly functional in its application, and I take it that the aim is to not to distract from the content. The lines are often short, with occasional movements towards something longer. There are times when a playful mood takes over and rhyme is used. And patches of prose occur here and there. It all emphasises the point I made earlier, that it's a complete work and not just a loose assemblage of poems which only have collective relevance because they were written by the same person.

There is something to be gained here if the reader takes the trouble to look for it. Amusing, entertaining, desperate, dis-illusioned, hopeful, regretful, sad, bitter, optimistic, pessimistic. What a mixture. And thoroughly human in its desire to deal with it all and stay alert to its possibilities.

—Jim Burns

Author's Preface

I have grouped the poems very loosely into chronological 'periods', even though, up until the Millennium, they are of a similar 'mixture' coloured by shades of life experience. (After that, the style is hopefully more consistent.) The poems may be read as a narrative. I am indebted to William Weiss for suggesting this structure, and to Jean-Paul L. Garnier for taking on the task of producing a Complete Poems volume.

My first poem, 'Authority', was written in anger at a teacher who caught me smoking. Aged fourteen, I wasn't angry at being caught – it's what you'd expect. I was enraged at the sneaky manner he employed to catch me. The poem is now lost, but it became a theme, and much of my life has been spent fighting abuses of power – in keeping with the age in which I grew up.

1965–1968

My early poems (aged seventeen to twenty-one), the surviving ones, were written from a background of wonderment and boredom, exploration and dissatisfaction with the slow progress I was making as a writer. Time seems to go too slowly, and stretches ahead infinitely. The sixties 'happening' on my doorstep fascinate me, and I try to make a difference for myself. The things that loom close are my just-completed six years at St Christopher boarding school, satirists like Rabelais and Cervantes and Jarry, the Beats (Burroughs and Kerouac), science fiction, Poe and concrete poetry. I am wary of overpopulation, the speed of technological change, the consumer society, environmental collapse and nuclear destruction. The things that interest me, other than books, are drugs, spaceflight, inner space, early psychedelia, hitchhiking to see friends in London. Auguries of death are never far away. I am by necessity a 'weekend hippy' and provincial, working at a polytechnic as a laboratory technician and living with my sisters and my mother in her lodging house in Altrincham, Manchester.

I have to pay my way. Commuting takes up a good deal of my time, also long solitary walks in Dunham and Bowdon, sexual fantasies (soon first sex). Equally potent are post-atomic war fantasies. I see clearly what is happening in the future, and record it, resulting in my first professional sale. Other transactions follow, and suddenly I am being feted as a young blood of the New Wave of Science Fiction. Callings of literary destiny, which are somehow related with a longing to go into space and the knowledge that one day I will do (I didn't, not factually) imbue me with an invulnerability that never entirely goes away. Grappling with this are feelings of uncertainty, trying to find myself. Terrible shyness and bodily un-coordination holds me back from full expression, but growing confidence that, somehow, I will be the next Edgar Allan Poe.

1968–1975
The setting now is of a deepening of life and an expanding awareness, of courtship, escape, marriage, children, growing up and compromise, but also of breakdown, feeling trapped, attacked, first divorce, reflection, trying to stop time, pining for a simpler past.

I am beginning a printing course (but drop out after one academic year), meet overseas students, become interested in politics, literary censorship and drug prohibition. ('Useless Black and White Sex Over Manchester'.) [In 1967 overseas students in the UK had their grants cut. Because the saving to the National Expenditure was relatively small the belief was widely held among students the cut was prejudicial. Many of the students were black and Asian. We marched together in solidarity.]

Sgt. Pepper's Lonely Hearts Club Band forms part of the backdrop. I undertake my first publishing ventures, and meet my first wife, G. London literary parties, Pink Floyd on Parliament Hill at night, working as a technician for Steiner Hair Products, praise and help from older writing peers. Make a new home for us in Radcliffe, and find new walking haunts in the semi-derelict North

Manchester industrial town. Serious relationship incompatibility ('Four Poems'). Dissociation, alienation, dispassion ('Builders of the Transpennine Motorway'). Our first child is born. Delighting in Nichola's birth and childhood I am able to see my own beginnings for the first time, knowing that before the miracle of her I was no more than a two-dimensional being skating about on the surface, aware of no one but myself and lacking depth. As I begin to see more something disconcerting happens. My early 'voice' as a writer disappears and becomes sporadic. Eventually it almost peters out. Rather like a painter suddenly starting to sculpt or film my urge to write is put into a different creative medium, publishing. I thought the world would see continuity, but it didn't. In literature, unlike art, you're either one thing or the other.

A second child is born, Damon. This one I watch leave his mother's womb, his birth another strange and wondrous thing. In 1974 America turns inwards, the moon landings cease, and brings to an abrupt end my youthful wishes and ideals. Now I am an advertising man, and take custody of our children. Feelings of being entombed. Awareness of limitations ('Breaking New Ground' and 'Poem Written as a Series of Statements') [the latter an experiment to see what restricting myself to short statements, a blank sheet of paper and no aforethought could produce], the first of my environmental poems ('Until Now'), but also disturbing marital breakdown reflections ('Five Connected Poems'*). Trying to still the rush to oblivion ('Autumn Poem'), though it is still 'early' and death is an infinitely impossible point to consider.

1975–1979

The props change. I am a single parent, a paperback writer. A new life starts for me. It is a 'middle' period. I look forwards, backwards and outwards. With my kids I move to the Harrow Road in London, near the cemeteries. On the one hand there is intense excitement. Complete my first novel, co-inaugurate the Savoy Books publishing house – our books will go all round the world. I am optimistic

---

* These poems do not form part of this collection.

('The Sitting Ducks', 'The New Man'), and have a new romance. But there is anger and sadness too. Taking my kids to and from school/nursery I observe a bag lady ('The Mad Girl'). [About a woman I passed each morning while wheeling my young son to his playschool at Queens Park, 'The Mad Girl' is a further experiment in restriction, limiting myself to writing short statements. As I hit the typewriter keys a rhythm starts, and the woman's story began to emerge.] It is a premonition of something very dark.

1979–1989

Disillusionment, gathering through the seventies, is complete as Margaret Thatcher [Trump-like] attempts to destroy all trace of my era's legacy. Her policies have a direct effect in the form of Manchester Chief of Police James Anderton, who begins a twenty-four-year war against my publishing house and bookshops. A conflict of values. A cultural war finds me a campaigner. As people around me conform, variously I am angry for literary freedom, weary, resigned, often bleak, even contemptuous ('Space Radio'). My first grandchild, Lianne, is born. The mood is both dark and light.

Authoritarianism. Bankruptcy. Prosecutions for obscenity by a policeman augur in an obsession with Hitler and the Holocaust that lasts until 1989 and a co-authored novel that is instantly seized by the Manchester police. A word crime, a dark pinnacle of the New Wave, it is celebrated and becomes the first book to be banned in England since *Last Exit to Brooklyn*. One of the things I do is hide away at Britannia Row Recording Studios with New Order, and begin the 'Blue Monday' diaries.

Having returned to my mother's house the demands of two young teenagers wear on her, necessitating a yearlong move to Hebden Bridge where I walk the crags, plot world domination and visit Sylvia Plath's grave in Heptonstall. At year's end the forty-two-year-old returns once again to his mother's house, but not all is the same. The relentless sweep of change swirls about the foundations of the base on which he has depended so merrily. As disturbing as anything in the decade's populist revolt, the childhood house is sold.

1989–2001

I am cut adrift. But while seduced by brief literary celebrity the reality of this severance does not impinge that much. It is a darkening undertow simply, and anyway I am soon caught up in the eddy of another maelstrom. I buy a house in Hadfield, at the foot of five reservoirs, the lowest and closest of which is called Bottoms ('Two Poems'). [The Longdendale Valley, to the east of Manchester has five reservoirs stepped up the valley. Bottoms is a five minutes walk from 17 Bankbottom, the Hadfield house where I lived when this poem was written. The novelist Hilary Mantel, I discovered, had spent her childhood at 56 and 58 Bankbottom. See her memoir *Giving Up the Ghost*.] For a few years I achieve domestic harmony with my children, hillwalking and holding Arthur Machen 'Dog and Duck' weekends. But new publishing ventures are in the air, and I am unable to resist hocking the house to pay for them.

A new court case finds me back in London. I have grown a beard, and am 'on the run' escaping possible imprisonment, and contemplate setting up a new publishing office in New York or London, anywhere away from the Manchester police. Discovering I am to be fined instead of imprisoned, I return to my home city. But unable to pay a second mortgage my Hadfield house is taken off me and sold. I move to apartments above the Arndale Shopping Centre, Manchester. In the high court I manage to get the ban on my book overturned, but not a ban on comics seized on a separate raid. My unsuccessful struggle to reverse the charge on these will go on for most of the decade.

My second grandchild, Sophie, is born. I begin clubbing, and take the music, the DJs, the opening up of sudden social horizons very seriously. A friendly romance is followed by an affair, and then another friendly romance. The Manchester IRA bomb goes off. I am made homeless with just the clothes I stand up in, and provided with temporary accommodation before being allowed back to Cromford Court … where (finally) fliering for my daughter Nicky's club night *Burst* I meet my forever partner.

Alas, S and I have found one another only just in time, for the locale now is death. In a short few years my mother is diagnosed with Alzheimer's, and dies. Sara is diagnosed with lupus, a chronic illness, and her beloved stepmother dies.

2001–2020

The poems, moments, that comprise this period of my life were originally to be titled *Poems of Death and Emptiness.* Such pieces were always to be found in my work, but scattered about. Now they are my mature style.

The backdrop is of increasing maturity as our new relationship deepens. The police raids are over. I have stopped fighting. We have become Buddhists ('Love Poem for S'). [S had returned from retreat at Tiratanaloka, having written love letters to me that I was unable to return due to retreat rules. I planted fresh bedding bulbs – miniature yellow narcissi – in the balcony planter to welcome her.] Anything but the actual present has been stripped back, and I look at death in the face, and see it is just change and flow.

Despite beatification, I am never far from a maelstrom. Civil unrest ('Off to the Riots!'). [The 2011 England riots, more widely known as the London Riots, were a series of riots between 6th and 11th August 2011, when thousands of people rioted in cities and towns across England. It saw looting, arson, and mass deployment of police, and the deaths of five people. From our balcony in Manchester we watched groups of young people making their way to the city centre, some drawn by curiosity but unsure of what they might find.] Even closer to home my daughter Nicky's family implodes, and Lianne and Sophie run away. My father ails, and is taken to hospital, eventually care homes, and dies. A disagreement with one of my sisters about his care becomes acrimonious and goes on until his death, spoiling the opportunity for all of us – including him – to take our leave.

There is war, or at least the centenary of it ('Gallant? For Fighting?'). [About the rise of nationalism in Europe after visiting a First World War Hospital re-enactment in the summer of 2014 during the centenary of war's outbreak. The minimal installations – comprising digital groans of 'wounded soldiers' in their 'beds' – evoked a sombre mood in the visitors. But something unexpected and shocking happened. Instead of feeling sadness for these imaginary patients I found myself overcome by horrified laughter at their stupidity. I told myself that some of these poor souls had been the not-too-bright victims of warmongers. But the laughter, accompanied by intense anger, boiling up inside me, would not go away. The longer I lingered the more the impulse to laugh out loud built up until, through fear of offending others, I left the room. As the wheel moves forwards it moves backwards, the next time perhaps fatally. The realisation that despite the promise of the intervening years since the forties when it seemed as though, after all the evidence to the contrary, we may finally be capable of change, that actually nothing has changed, that we may be incapable of change, that it is war as usual, led to my outburst.]

With encouragement from Sara, I start writing seriously again, and launch new publishing imprints. She is ordained and in my poems becomes 'M' (Moksavadini, 'she who speaks of liberation'). My sister dies, the obstreperous one, leaving only one sister and myself (the eldest) out of our family of five. Time has now done a funny thing. It's become very fast. Linearity has gone. I am no longer dissatisfied.

1965−1968

•

You're moving through life
Turning things off turning things on
Planning
Arranging
Deciding
Getting in the way of truth

'truth' is just being –
not trying.

Author in his room at night

I fancy outsiders
Must see a wreck of vodka.
They cannot tell
He writes poetry for them –
Short of breath – and of a girl
Who has gone away to the sea in Wales

the nose

he simply laid out his hand
on the girl's face
then her nose forced a way through his fingers into
the stratosphere where it blew itself
violently into the clouds and menaced supersonic aircraft

Michael Butterworth

•

The deep warm
Immersed you in
Summer grass

•

Unfinished
Flashes of cloudscape
Lie between the
Summer houses. Clouds
Rush back from the street
Into a high and evaporated vacuum.
Identity is swopped.
I am a pylon
That curves its steel
Into the centre of the
Sunny drift: vaporous
Stringvest of pale
Tints likening
To the seashell patterns
Of dreams

over a neon city

over a neon city
i flew once to inspect
a sewage works

i flew back disgusted
because nothing in life
seemed to fit properly

after flitting around
burning buses and
smashing down fences
and crying
i sat in a smoke-filled room
all night and played cards

brass life

her legs
shot her over a mountain
just for me

though her eyes were like
the glazed eyes
trapped in buses
she passed me by

i had the courage
and undid my fly
she spread her
petrolwarmth through me
i thought of filling stations

The Legacy (spoken by King Trash in 2030)

In later times, it became so bad for these ancients
That they had no GO in them.
After leaving childhood for good
They didn't climb up the ladder
But fell down and broke their legs,
Wherever they looked
They saw shit. Whenever they bent down
They got hooked. Wherever they went they
Arrived back at the beginning. Whenever they
Arrived back at the beginning, they went.
To cap it all they often looked into the
Guts of the world and turned away puking.
If they looked anywhere
They saw some commercial drunkard
Had been sick. The obvious outcome
Is plain to me. At one stage
Things and people shat on one another. Then
The rockets were called in –
And I've got the legacy.

after galactic war — from a road on earth

the road wound along under the night sky
set in the sky
were the crystals of the ships that had been broken
each chip was a silent
last fleck of humanity
together with the vanity of the ground
which bent up to meet them the
space beyond buckled inwards under the
pressure of the true stars and
sandwiched the chips into bars of space music

they needed no air
were archaic flowers off the rings of all dead girls
gems centred the jewelled scene into curls
in the front of my head.
i looked out of the forehead
of a doubledecker bus
and my legs were wheels
i rolled over the pitted road pickpocketing the night
i rode the night like a baby stalk lost in Heaven
not seven anymore
wondering why

In Willian Fields

The white moon
is the night's bestseller
selling the
flower fields of the
house-black countryside

The tree-shadowed
cork church
strikes,
sending
a rolling bell meadow
across the moon

The financier of the elm
is the clear-cut
orb in tailored
white
paying the elm twigs
dust

Its tooth-white
is the dentist

The bole of the
elm harbours the spaceships
of the cornfields
which climb
from one moon to another

Paula

Paula pronounced Powla
Visited some time ago.
Finnish we called Lapp,
The longhaired blonde
Of the Finnish roads blue
Very pale eyes
With a moonlike smile
Pretended no knowledge of our language
And sat on her own drinking tea forever
Calling Finnish tea and listening to our talk

hoover & writer

it sucks up
the stairs from
room to room
cleaning the guts
out of indispensable furniture

doors open and
close
lessening and increasing the
sound of its hunger

thoughts
of importance
fly away
into its desensitising mouth

it spits out the rubbish
and takes up the words
and then it
clatters away
down the stairs

leaving an awkward
blob
of silence

girl hitchhiker (for c)

you came off the road out of the avenues of
receding red lights with your dog smoky like a surprise
animal come to wake me from my writing
and started a revolution in my skull

My Bed is Too Short

Surely, when they bury me they will think of my legs,
Long tapering devices,
So mechanical I hardly notice.
Perhaps they'll bury me in my bed.

Michael Butterworth

Useless Black and White Sex Over Manchester

the banners in the
        Oxford Road today
                say 'Black Brain Drain'
      coloured red-on-white cloths
            supported by sticks
   still they stilt along
in the hands and the
         minds of 2,000 students
      who arrived to study under the grey clouds
        in the rain
the column forges into the rain
     is the column
     a cobra slithering
     on the tarmac a
     black advance into England?
  each hand for each banner
        is angry
          and each head is a hand pulling
     worthless rupees
       out of bad pockets
   the poor "angry brown men"
     erupt into the sun
       behind the cloud
  fingers that thrust
  once more
       into the Phynance of England
– give them their education –
    – saved are £5,000,000s of blue notes of
     piggy savings –
the banners in the Oxford Road
    held to the crumpled faces
     of the public

and the distorted minds of the Press
hold up black and
white sex in the sky
and unsolicited
evoke the faded image of
Queen Victoria
her long reign of her dying eyes
– the years are in the weeds –
her twinkle in the pompoms
and the opium dens
of the New Worlds
black voices are our
only white hearts
the palpitations to a false set-up
the false Ministry of Democracy
it is hid somewhere
in Skakespeare's tomb
where it is explicit writ
"do not disturbe these
bonies from the stonies"
– President de Gaulle
or some similar
is author to our democracy –
the banners in the wet
shiny Oxford Road
reflecting at least
(for one last time)
the feet of Overseas
perhaps in our Ministry's eye
the cobra of tones
surges
blows its horn in

                        the angry traffic
              it might just as well
                    be Oxford Street
                              London
                        England 1914
                    Nagasaki
                        Auschwitz
                    Hiroshima
              or Carnaby Street
            England
                    out of your flies your friends
      and your brains fly
              and this useless
                        black and white sex in the sky
                    above Manchester
                        is a prophecy
                              a prediction
                        of your present state

Circularisation of Condensed Conventional Straight-line Word-image Structures (Radial-planographic Condensed Word-image Structures, Rotation About a Point)

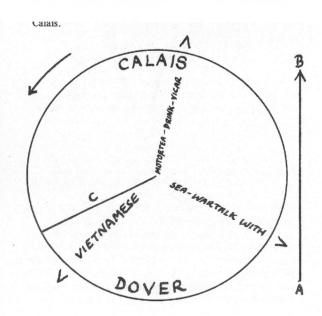

Take:

I crossed the channel, Dover to Calais, in a motorboat. I had a drink of tea on the way.

Condense:

Dover sea motortea-drink Calais

Take:

I crossed the channel, Dover to Calais, in a motorboat. I had a talk about the war in Vietnam with a vicar, over a drink of tea.

Condense:

Dover. Vietnamese sea wartalk with motortea-drink vicar. Calais.

15

No Truce at White Holocaustmas-time
(Year of crossing – 1967)

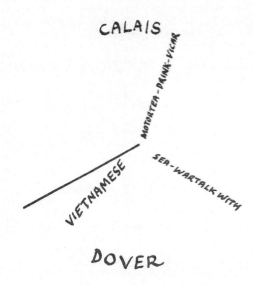

VICAR:
Against background noise of sea and boat. War, Vietcong soldiers,
   civilians, are for most of us simply images, not reality.
NARRATOR:
Ah, but what's Reality? Who can define that, Vicar?
VICAR:
I…

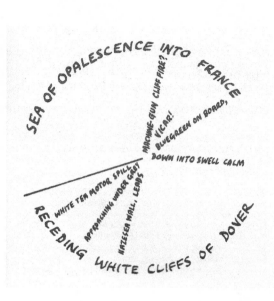

NARRATOR:

Against background noise of motorboat and sea. Ah, yes Reality!
Those white cliffs. Good tea, isn't it?

VICAR:

Oops! All over you, sorry. This reminds me of a long time ago, on
the sea in a small boat. Or was it a book I'd been reading, about
a hunchback who operated a ferry service across the Channel?
He used a rowing boat, by the way, and rescued trapped soldiers
from the beaches at Dunkirk.

NARRATOR:

I can almost hear the machine-gun fire coming from the cliffs. It's
almost like Thomas Hardy now…

VICAR:

Reality? We're over board into fantasy in a minute! *Sound of
machine-gun fire in the distance.*

VICAR:

Reality? In this case a process of… of friendly permutation of first impressions. If soldiers did really encounter Reality, instead of the propagandised Image of 'hatred' their respective governments cloak around The Enemy, they would not fight!

NARRATOR:

We'll soon be in Calais. What are you going to do once we get there?

VICAR:

I have a friend…

Frame 3

VICAR:

Against background noise of sea and boat. This is precisely what I mean. They're human now, true Christians, filled with brotherly spirit. For the rest of the year they fought one another. Can you believe it, seeing them so happy now? *Sounds of laughter and merriment coming from the trenches.* Christmas in Vietnam. You remember? They did the same thing.

NARRATOR:

At what cost? Look, if only you can, at my remembrances. There
is a man…

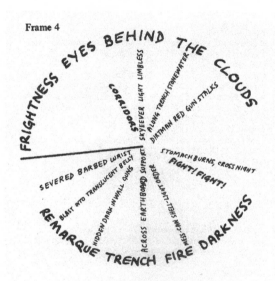

Frame 4

NARRATOR:

*Against background noise of 1st WW machine guns, trench groans,
sea and motorboat.* Now you see what I mean about War.

VICAR:

I see pain and suffering. I see no motive, only an exchange of
senseless attacks. If men met in the flesh, instead of reading
newspapers about one another, as they did last Christmastime,
they would soon learn not to hate one another. Because of a
humanising element that both sides have in common – a love
of Father Christmas, if you like. Image of War, go away back
into the clouds.

NARRATOR:

And of War? Isn't War just a *word?* We're getting onto very vapourous ground; here Vicar, finish your tea. Water water everywhere and it's all salt! How I suffer.

Frame 5

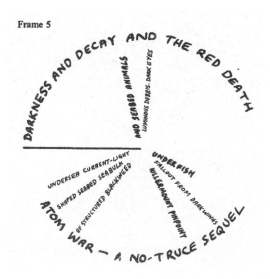

VICAR:

Ah, the French coast, clearly at last. Listen to what they say – the white cliffs ten miles behind. *Very loud 'rat-tat' of machine-gun in echo chamber.* But there will be no question of postatomic survival. We'll have fought so much hatred to do that. It'll not be a question of slipping across the lines to have a mixed party... Enemy prejudice – false superboosted hatred Images – won't exist. *Sound of motorboat and sea comes suddenly into the foreground, as if the wind changes.*

VICAR:

Shouting above the noise. I have a friend who runs a church in
   Versailles…

Frame 6

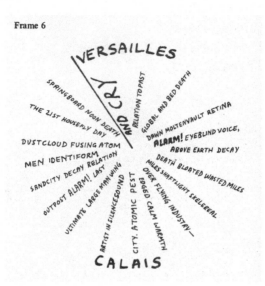

*Sound of motorboat and sea. In the distance, bells and cannons
   from* 1812 Overture. *Silence.*

●

the dawn of man
and man has taken
smoked sniffed absorbed…
injection is a modern thing
injection is quickest to the brain
he has drunk
starved and flayed his body
it's all the same

Sergeant Pepper's Postatomic Skull

Part 1

this must be the last time I shall speak to anybody… i can speak
but i can speak to no *body*… there is no mind to speak to…
there is no machine to sate the vacuum of desire left in my
skull for a mechanical aid… *any* mechanical aid no matter how
simple in structure or in ease of appliance would suffice…
there is no advert to fill the vacuum… there is no recollection
but what i can recall is confused and garbled like the effects of
a hallucinogen
how it all started… how did it all start… why write anything…
why bother… once a man has had his skull cracked and brutally
soddened with a heavy kick he is not there… his mind… his
body… has gone… the universe revolves ceaselessly… the
drug is on the table where the man left it… the ant crawls… the
advert flickers…
this must be a rooming house in Manchester where i had an affair
with a girl who turned into a rocking horse… sergeant peppers
lonely hearts club band is playing… the music seems an
endless tide of memories – *it momentarily filled the vacuum
and brought a smile to her face* – the shadows of other people
lay across the carpet sat smoking in green wicker chairs their
loneliness a mere measure of the vacuum that now occupied
every skull –
'it's funny but when you smoke everything goes you let everything
go you can't do that with alcohol' –
the girl walked amongst tangerine trees under a marmalade sky in
a land of cellophane flowers –

'THE GIRL WITH KALEIDOSCOPE EYES' –

this must be a place in my mind

the circular music –
i thought of a plastic disc revolving
i thought of the amassed creativity cycle
of the artists involved
i thought of the publicity cycle... the girl
is boosted and is accepted is accepted which accepts is boosted
i listened to a day in the life and came across the ending to a filling
    that never
existed...
i know what this place is now this place out here on the agoraphobic
    slopes... the postatomic area where the bomb explodes because
    of the vacuum... i hear the aftermath silence of a storm as the
    record finishes... a ringing brain that listens to the show that
    only noise will take away... and now there is no noise but
    this paranoia speeding everything up... my thoughts return to
    a same origin as the needle traps itself in the groove of the
    missing line... it is quiet... it is all apparent... understandable...
    everything is clear at last... now you know what life is about...
you are a waxwork

Part 2

in my skull
is the triangle
of today's lies
the unrealities
in my hand
should be the land
one point of the triangle lies unfixed in space... a point
determined from day to day... a capsule falls... the hypotenuse
    is its track until it hits the sea or land and is rescued from the
    silent vacuum of space – the silent vacuum of the mind... the

points that complete the figure lie buried in stage props with invisible roots in the earth going down to hell

the astronaut is paraded along the streets of the city whilst the capsule travels through his mind its journey never over... he raises an arm to the crowds and a cracked smile... it has been a long journey... too long he complains... adverts assail the empty sea he's brought back with him... in his head he lifts another arm to ward off the reflected glare of the faces of the crowd... he is blinded by his own image... boosted on gigantic structures that have no meaning... his automatic eye is suddenly back in the stars where his skull belongs

in hell on earth... intersect the orbit entry line with the stabilising base at a point where the sun's rays hit the earth – a globe placed at the end of a cold photon passage through space... a hotplate of plants and animals

'the best place in the universe' says the astronaut

where rain from a cloud can be seen to strike a liquid where a breeze from the air pushes a cloud too far and a man is wet where animals eat animals and plants where plants eat animals

'this competition has been forgotten' the astronaut tries to say... he wishes he was on another planet... he draws a nail from his eye and fuses this into his thumb where it belongs... a skeleton of iron and a skin of cardboard he takes leave of the pressmen and walks into the precincts to escort his wife's baby into another world

in hell on earth... intersect the orbit exit line – the hypotenuse – with the stabilising base –

the third point is where the hypotenuse intersects the brain... a collage of wasted portraits... so many words and a vacuum formed that stops the astronaut dead in his tracks

his hand on the end of a bank loan his payment to cross the sea AND THE BIRDS DO IT FREE... *he is some kind of messiah returned from space to preach to the crowds...* he dreams that night he is riding the hypotenuse again ever returning from his mind... he dreams he is on another planet while the adverts flicker in his brain threatening that if he does his own transposed personality in the vacuum of space will change... and so will his dreams... an automobile drives through his eyes

Part 3

mr kite is nameless
who are the hendersons
why are they famous
who is billy shears
are the beatles a reality
in the vacuum of space – the black inner space of mind – caused by the slow interstellar bombardment of returning image... is a case of having to increase the dose... and there is never enough... in the vacuum it is allowed

edgar poe – an unreal character who should be dead – is there... out of a big modern novel... with the eyes of his blind conqueror worm a serpent that shifts from one gaze to the next living off borrowed image at the age of forty... his youth is distant and irrepairable and lived-in like a cinema

the worm does not know where to turn what to do… it destroys
  the false – yet it is fled from and destroyed… it destroys –
  the scenes collapse and also the dependent mind in an orgy of
  self-destruction… mr kite flies through the ring on a fanfare
  of trumpets… the rest stampede in panic into the black from
  the worm within which will now eat the whole head and leave
  the clothes of the victim in de-imagined shreds… streaming
  colours flash by in a blur into the vacuum… seen yet unseen…
  the heated liquids of
marlon brando
diana dors
bob dylan
joan crawford
marilyn monroe
stan laurel
frank sinatra
w c fields
oliver hardy
the beatles
e a poe
the liquids freeze inside… a shapeless mass of waxen image
  imageless at last and freed of the circular track… there is no
  colour in the dark… the record is circular

a product… the drug tract needling the vacuum that is like that
  other vacuum that surrounds the earth… the drug is circular…
  it fills the whole vision of the skull till the skull loves it…
  cannot empty itself quick enough of image that is five days old
  and grabs at every loose end that is meaningful to its imagined
  existence

i cannot seem to find words that will convey meaning what use are words but the niceties of a race best left out of this place where this place is in the postatomic area... where the bomb explodes because of the emptiness where there is no smell no sense to staying but to lessen the vacuum... i hear the aftermath silence of a storm as the record finishes... a ringing brain that listens to a dying show that only noise will take away... there are no words... there is no advert to fill the vacuum... there is no recollection... sometimes there is recollection but what i can recall is confused and garbled as if somehow i could if i tried be the ultimate cynic out here on the postatomic slopes

An ode to collage artists

a way out of the houses
and cars and
female busts and
cut up cunts
hidden by hands and
replaced with teeth and
crossed with cables and
seen through shades
stuck on a road

no sky in these pictures
(cut out by mad
collage artists and
replaced with bumpers and headlights
from a 1970 Cadillac)
no sky way out
(startling welter of vari-
energised articles used to
bathe and work the brain leave
the page – can
this thing here
really be a human being
or is it a customised doll?)

i see a way out! with
a Kent cigarette! –
a piece of sky trapped
beneath a bust of
George Harrison
…perhaps
it can be got into and out of

the importance of me

i understand immeasurably
the importance of me
that in the land
i have a percentage tree
built of sand
regulating the pound

．

one day
a man opened
   a can
out jumped a gold watch
                  what have I done
                  what have I done
you have been found guilty of stealing a gold watch
said the judge
for this you must be punished
you bet
said 56 coppers
and when you have been punished
continued the judge
you will be set
free
again

Girl in Bath

She rises out of the water
By her thighs
Feeling the tinkling loss of herself

The likeness

i am
in the universe
and
i am myself
and
i see a
reflection of
myself
in every person

and
in every
person there is
a reflection
of me
and
in every person   but it is
there is   my
a universe   image
and   i deal in
i contain   when i
a universe and   deal with
i am a   people
universe   and
and   my image
in every person   is reflection
there is   and
a universal me   people *are*
             by reflection
             and when
             i
             deal in image
             i
             must make
             a clean deal
             "your
             image for my
             image"

Farness

there is a scene
happening over
the question of tea
'there's no food in
the house' from
the kitchen
'haven't we got any
thing in?' from
the living room
'NO!' peering round
the connecting door
'oh' getting up
why does it take two
people, he
thinks, to say 'oh no'

later that night it
comes to him there is
nothing inside his head worth
thinking about and
worse
why talk about it? His
wife is asleep in
another bed in
another room somewhere in
their house remote
in her isolation

at three in the morning he
enjoys the nerves of
the night town in his
dressing-gown his

mind a tiny star as
he treads its tarmac
oh, he thinks to
himself very cautiously
oh, and *no*

icicle the tricycle and the letter box

icicle the tricycle went out to work one day
and came across a letter box that tried to block her way
she yanked her chain and pulled it off
and slung it at the letter box
which backed away and showed its teeth
a thousand letters at her feet
she picked them up and read the first
that told of bill the soldier nursed
in bed with bullet wounds inside his head

in a land of sand
in a faraway place
without any face

Concentrate 3

Space is communication. To a human being space is realisation. No
  imagination could. But the awareness of himself on a planet in
  the universe is psychedelic.
Matter measures time. Having experienced the highways of space
  and seen the stars and below him the planet earth…?

The Astronaut

Oceans of scrambled knowledge are in his head – they form a
  conflict between awareness and balance. Space scrambles his
  mind.
His suit protects him from the real cold and the real vacuum. But
  his confused mind (accustomed to a keen perception of space/
  time) flips.
Space became claustrophobic – suddenly there was no space, no
  time…
'Get his hat off.'
The struggling body was brought through the hatch into the station
  boarding bay. An attendant wearing a white gown removed the
  casualty's headpiece.
His head became hot and buzzed.
'The stars…'
He tried to say there was nothing but the stars crawling over his
  face, as though he found himself suddenly drowning in space.
'You became disorientated. All this talk about "highways of space"
  and "connections"…'
'No! There were unknown trillions…'

Valve

avenues of space of
spiralling currents
of low pressure ran
within the vacuum

fields of gravity
wakes of magnetic
debris called the hip
astronaut into line

his mind was filled up
with the works of man

he was a technical
part of the capsule

one country's gain of
name over another's

they led his frail
pressurised head into
the regions of low
pressure
and emptied it

•

a million light years from here
on a planet's
dusty floor a
rocket
drips
blood
from a wounded tail

Highlights of a Ten-minute Conversation
   Between Two Girls

1.

On your garden? In your house? With your car? Your cat? Your
                                              living room.
It's no excuse. It's a sweet. There's no water in the sink.
                                              Some pans.
They go on don't they? Not so much – it's the extra one.
            Still, it's great.
            Just don't take any notice. He knows.

2.

The children all say that! It's going to be even hurt. I know.
            She's funny, her.

under the influence of bush

1.

Reality is wonderful, how i
long for that glorious reality again

2.

He knew he was going to die
this became obvious straight away
there was a bright light in the sky
over his head

Birds poisoned with insecticide
flew in the sky
and landed on the desert
he tried to concentrate on their falling

Next door
a man was teaching chemistry
dropping little messages
he tried to listen to the clear words

He shivered in the heat
and drew his coat round his thudding heart
and tried not to think

two poems

1.
stamen protruding stick
y insect-catching prick
eighteen pricks rise into
the sun and listen
                 petals ope
                 n trail rope
                 y green climb
                    to the sun
flowers grow on the prow
of the cop's prowl boat
it push
es aside
the rush
es as it
       search
   es
      the marsh
es for drugs

2.
there's no blood
inside my skull
there's a blue sea –
                 water holly hocks
       yellow
            dandy lions
                  beneath the level sur
                  face face the sun
and in the gloom
on the bottom of the sea
i've no fun

                    and
                    on the ground in
          side
                    the power house
                    on land near
            by
                    the stream in
          side
                    the black doors
                    on the river side
        a dark seed
                            pod
                                        grows
        it flies in the sky!

three poems

1.
death feels
      brings
        up a couple of steps
brings the flesh in tiny shudders
drops away
curtains drawn from a window
suddenly
the skull tipping away its mind

2.
tiny whorl
tender wheels evolve
and
revolve,
mount nigel
and feels his world

small stoned flash
long black hair
makes for the whorl
headfirst
    and clenched fist

ends heaped…
convulsions –
wormlike forms

3.
against my will
i have set my
mind on dying

whatever i can do
to prevent my death
won't come off now

i have not realised
my desire before now
it is so simple
i want to die
before my mother dies

my mother meant
everything to me
i came from her
in her reign
she squeezed me out
in her reign
i shall die from her
my mother earth

in the blaze of night
i am terrified
i can just stand
up to it

i stand alone
in a forest of trees
kissing sanity

each tree
disintegrates
above my head
casts down a
shower of badly
remembered
pieces into the
calm water
at my feet

Misophonia

triclops rests his head
   smiles
   leers
brokenboned creature…

his wife
   rests in an armchair
after the satisfying meal
   burping
making little
   satisfied
     noises
idiot

the same noises
for a thousand years
  are beginning
    to depress triclops

upstairs he sits
on his bed and
stares at the wallpaper
  a thousand
    lightyears away…

his spaceship
  rests in his head
it revolves
  slowly in his mind
    a dinky toy…
he puts it

between his legs
and points it upwards

a line of black…
he is seeing
the universe edge-on
   the ship
      revolves infinities of
         awareness before his eyes
      glints of sunlight
come from behind his eyes

1968–1975

for gina

emotion engulfs
me when I have you
or merely
when we kiss
each cell wants to join
become one thing

when we're apart
adrift i
feel a vacuum
an infinity of need
tearing apart the cells

Michael Butterworth

The Builders of the Transpennine Motorway

as for him,
i suppose
he knows
how long
it took
to build a road
running from
A to B
over really
rough
country

suprising
he doesn't
come out
now
and say
a thing
or two
about the weather
in these
hilly parts

heavy hilly
rain drowns
them all

red iron
mud cakes
their boots

natural oil
sticks to
their souls

special
mountain winds
blow their
cheeks raw

hands
them down
into the
valleys and
plains like
shot crows

maybe he's
sleeping at
this time
of the
year and won't
be caught
by anyone

nothing will
rouse him

even the
beautiful
wife of
one driller

is in
bed at
this time

but for
him i
doubt if she
really cares
really

they have
a hell
of a time
working
in those
tunnels
and chancing death
like that

operating
large
machinery
that might
go wrong

they all
want a
good meal

Four Poems

1.
One
wife
stays out at
nights with
out her
husband
anymore

'I'm taking
a rest at
my sister's tonight
because of my health
ever since
I met you
it's been going
rapidly
down hill

'I'm sick
and tired
of being told
what to
do and
where to
go by you
I need a rest!'

all the
pots and
pans
dirty in

the kitchen
sink his
smelly socks
dirty
on the bedroom
floor his
dirty shirts
in every
crack and hole

her untidiness
everywhere
half-finished bits and
pieces her
child-like
reality no
tea when
he comes
home she's
out of work

'I need a
rest I'm going round
to a friend's
see you'

2.
'I'm not
spending
the rest of
my life

with you
knowing
he loves
you and you
love him
why can't
you tell
me? Do
I have
to thought-
read you
all the time?
Whether
you know
it or
not we as
husband
and wife
don't make
it we
can only
exist together
now that
your gap
has been
filled and
you have
no further
use for me
he loves
you so
why not

go with him?
You see
I don't
want a
predicament
where I
provide your
house your
car your
material
purpose
in life
and you
are forced
to have
your lover'

3.
This is just to confirm
that I've paid the rent
collected the groceries
washed the pots
made the evening meal
scrubbed out the toilet
swept the stairs
washed the socks and soaked the bras
paid the milkman
seen to the cat's meal
emptied the garbage can
turned on the television

sewed the hole in your jeans
mended the electric fire
put money in the meter
run the bathwater
borrowed milk from the neighbours
borrowed money from the bank
borrowed bus fare from work
got you the interview with IBM
run to the doctor's for you
changed the sheets
hoovered the living room carpet
made the breakfast
tidied the bedroom
hung up your coats
folded your dresses
nursed your illnesses
got you to night school
changed the sheets
prepared the laundry
finished my latest story

4.
The phone rings.
'Darling. I'm in a fix.'
'Not again.'
'Look, it's really bad this time. I don't know how I'm going to
    manage.'
'What've you gone and done this time…'
'It's Damon, I just can't go on…'
She sobs, crackling down the line. Is she sobbing, or is she laughing?
'Look, what can I do to help? I'm busy.'

'I don't know. You must think I'm stupid. Don't think I don't hate myself for doing this to you... I've got no one else to turn to. Since we bust up I can't...'

She is crying harder now. Is it a put on?

'I'm afraid there's nothing I can do... I can't keep intervening in your life. I've got my own problems to sort out. Besides, I'm broke. And there's John...'

'I see.'

'I don't mean to be *hard,*' I say more softly. 'Surely you can understand?'

Silence.

'Look, I'm very busy... you phoned at the wrong time. See how it goes, eh? Phone again.'

'OK.'

She is quiet now. The sobbing has gone. She is sorry she phoned, holding it all in. I can tell. I feel sick inside. But she can't let the receiver go.

'OK. 'Bye now,' I force my voice neutral and level, not wanting to show any emotion at all until after the divorce.

The Builders of the Transpennine Motorway: Part 2

even
over
hungry hills
he does
not wake
sufficiently
to release
them
from their tasks

his drilling
mechanisms
are hypnotic

their
routines
take them
further
into the
mountain face
than man
has
ever bawd

they
control
their tools
with
old familiarity
like
their wives

endless
chatter
into the rock face
with
their
hard-pricking
drills

it
takes
quite some
men
to hold
all that
noise

Waste Paper

Waste paper
Don't make it.
If you got waste paper,
Chew it, burn it, bury it.
Don't drop it.
Don't spit it out.
Get rid of the evidence.
Let it drop, and that's the end.
You won't make it.
It isn't hip to drop litter.
Hold litter to your hip.

•

•

this new life
such an old 'me'

On Broken Hill
Where Awful Bill
Broke Princess Jill
A black car waits.
"This is the house,"
Says Vernox the Mouse
"Where Jillian lies.
Hear her cries?"
He cups a hand.
"The Devil's land!"
The three men wait
In the black estate,
Ejaculate.

Illusion

Sometimes, you can see her face,
Deep in the mirror.
She lives in the same room as I,
Separated by glass.

•

When I walk, I bounce one vertical mile.
Heads turn. Eyes look.
It's impossible, getting through this gauntlet,
And dreaming about it at night
And now I'm trapped. Grounded. Floundering in the low water,
Caught by their stares, which bind me like seaweed.
Individual strands snap easily,
But when thousands
Intertwine with each other...

We walk along the seas-shore, my granny and I,
A kindly, grey-haired old lady
Who explains how the bones that
Litter the beach
Arrived in her bay.
"One day, last summer, a shoal of whales,
Mostly young, were grounded
By a storm.
Several men from the village
Tried to refloat them,
But to no avail.
The poor creatures were crushed by their own weight."
I look down at the white, bleached pieces of myself,
And wonder how they felt before they died.
I could not escape the storm.
Dying was unavoidable.

•

The buildings are very low round here,
Built into the earth.
Surely the occupants must suffer badly
Getting in and out through these half-filled doors?
The air is to blame,
Heavy with lead smokes
Pressing the roofs of the buildings into the earth.
Quite honestly, I wouldn't like to live round here.
My children would be poisoned.
The sunken houses are warning us:
"Don't come. Don't come."

•

Here comes the train
late again
the half-past nine
the weather is fine
hold up
on the line.
My young pup
was living fine.
He got knocked
on the line
socked
by the diesel
the ten to nine.
A kestrel
flies high
above the line.

The weather is fine.

•

My Gina
Georgina
She's the sweetest gal
I ever knew
She makes me feel
Like Vegetable stew
She's the greatest cook
You ever met
She's a real good marm
I'm bound to bet
She's a writer
And a poet
A fighter
An' she know it
She got style
All the while
She got taste
Fish paste
The best thing about her
She's a real good lover
We make it together
Like birds of a feather
An' our daughter
From love's water
Is born
Forlorn
Quiet as a cloud
She isn't loud
Nichola's her name
And ends love's game

•

1.

After all the words, nothing… the most intense vacuum. A few
white clouds in the sky, turning grey, suddenly not seen. There
is no cat on the floor turning its head one way then another.
There is no clock, ticking, on the mantelpiece, above the gas
fire. There is no carpet, lying on the floor…
…no floor.
No walls,
or ceiling.
There is no sound,
no colour,
taste, or smell. No touch.
No hearing, there is no breathing, or movement.
No life…

2.

After I am fully awake I discover
my head – it has grown enormously
during the night. My artificial limbs,
screwed-off last night by Gina, they
are no longer there – in their place
I feel great loss. There are no
warm hands to touch my thighs or soft
lips to pick my eyes. I have grown
quite cold. My head has been pulled
out of the motionless river by the
yachtsmen. It lies white and swollen
on the wooden planks at the bottom of
the boat. When I've left that cold
world, and inquisitively pressed them,
its eyes release water.

Daffodil

My head was a daffodil. I was a plant of winter. Snow fell on
me from time to time and ice grew round my roots.

I had good feet for walking and a strong back to support me.
My wrists were like iron and gripped a rose. My arms
were dark timbers. They ended in coal fingers. I was used as a fire
shovelled from a coal shed to warm a lounge.

My heart was a pencil writing its name on a torn piece of card-
board hanging from a railing in a car park.

My feet were cement that crumbled to dust in libraries of reading
books. They walked on an antelope's grave by a city stream
polluted with chemicals.

My fingers held the key to a safeful of matches with green heads
that burst into flames when the lock was picked.

My head was a battleground. It was bleeding from a hole in its
side where the muzzle of a tank pointed out.

•

Wounded in the flesh
By years of sorrow.
Love for himself
Produced the
Worst barbs.

For G

Once upon a time, ugly duckling,
a *long* time ago,
did you see that place for you
waiting in the world?
You knew who you'd be,
knew what you'd do
when you grew up, now
grown up and sat over there
in the shadows crying.

Somehow it all went wrong,
didn't it, duck?
Your high-ideas were
scoffed at, you weren't
even allowed to try them out.
You were all wrong,
the other ducks were right:
wasn't that how
they made you feel?
Ugly?
Duck?

Well, I know you *tried*
to join in the games,
but after a while
it was all pretence,
wasn't it?
You *tried* to earn their love
but no one did,
did they? And after a lot of
heartache you
left the ducks who

stole your place
peeping at you
from behind curtains
in the cozy cottage
by the bubbling brook
in the countryside
at Ringway with
the three kids
and happiness,
and realised you had
to hate them
and that's
just what you do
don't you, ugly duck?

There comes a point
in the fairytale though
when the ugly duck
finds friends
and flies off with the swans.
From then on
you are a swan all along,
beautiful to look at, knowing what you want
all over again.

Premature

1.
The planet's dusty surface has been scratched
with a handful of probes
and a few manned expeditions.
A plain, some craters, and a mountainous region
have been explored.
                    Science has prospered.

Aesthetes have not been surprised, for they have
known in advance what strange worlds are like.

The lay mind has accepted with disbelief
information that does not concern it.

America has a feather in her cap. Russia has always
considered that a long-term expedition to Mars
is better meat than a famine in the land.

2.
Mankind is benefited, but
no use has been seen yet for
escaping men. They can solve no hunger problems,
no land disputes. They can find no homes for
homeless families, nor cure pollution.

Minerals still abound on earth in plenty,
and the threat from overpopulation
is a comfortable ride in the future:
so the moon's offerings go unheeded.

3.

America stops the race. So little
of the planet has been
discovered. Launch pads are sold, jobs are lost: America prefers
    her
Vietnam, and repairs are needed to the holed economy.
Her people militate for a better quality of living.

To the rest of the world, the astronauts will become
ghosts, men who walk on the moon, parts in a cunning
simulation trick performed by politicians. In time,
they will be resurrected, or Russia, or a combined
industrial effort will add dimension to the fiction.

Michael Butterworth

Poem written as a series of statements

Wind whistles through leaves…
Dusky grey evening…
Rooftops line the horizon in lines of black cut-outs…
Trees sway in the wind…
Rain slants through the sky from rolling clouds…
Barbed wire hems-in the trees, nailed to their unfeeling trunks…
Round the copse rolls a hectacre of crops, flattened by the rain…
    Emergency supply trucks trundle across the landscape…
Still the wind rises…
Rain lashes at the roofs…

She smiles at me from the 4-poster where we made love a moment
                                                 ago…
She rises from the bed and flings out her arms and stands flat-
                            breasted astride her tuft…
Rain rolls down the windowpane…
Sperm slides down her belly…
Still the wind cries, howling round the rafters…
Soot slides down the chimney, hits the back of the gas fire and
                crackles above the low recording coming from the
    deck…
Candle light stands on the mantelpiece, a white stick of dripping
                                    tears…
Little wax faces fall away onto the hearth…

Next, a picture of a small shanty hut with a beaten earthen floor…
A squaw sits naked on her haunches fingering her clout…
A rat scuttles across the hardened earth…

We slip out of the hut holding hands, two naked links in a biologic
                                         chain…

We slip through slim shadowy birch stems painted a dull metallic
silver in the moonlight…
We tread naked across natural lawns clipped smooth by deer teeth,
our bodies bathed in cosmic light…
The natural light refreshes our skins and recharges our organs…
The cool, trembling nearness of the plants heals my scars…
She looks at me without a wrinkle on her forehead…
Now she is free of worries and unfettered, nothing nags at her mind…
Like this, I could always be with her…
We roll down on the cool grey lawn…
Grey sealskins in the moonlight…
A flood of sperm pumps deep inside – a lifetime's agony, cleansed…
She lies slain on the grass shaking her head from side to side
ecstatically mouthing sounds that never issue forth…
The ground is hard and firm, the flesh is soft and weak… life forms
trapped in biologic suits writhe about in pleasure and in pain,
their lives a series of crests and valleys…
Outside, mountains slide…
Comets fly…
Planets crunch…
The wind rises…

The convoy reaches the border, held back by the clay churned up
from the endless
furrows…
Dying surface vegetation slips away as wind and rain slash at the
ground…
I smell the rotten smell of the mushy stems pervading everywhere…
No chink is small enough to hide in to escape their repugnance…
The convoys arrive too late to help the village…
Bodies lie white and bleached by the rain, slipping into the endless
mud…

Michael Butterworth

Space Radio still broadcasts from the orbiting space station high
            above the Earth, its signals less frequent and getting
      worse...
Maybe we are the only survivors...

I stand naked, angry, frightened in the wood...
Old familiar feelings burn over me, feelings I thought I had done
                              with long ago...
I let go the lifeless head in my grip and bring the murdering hands in
      front of my eyes, barely visible in the dark... I see the intense
            presence of the trees spaced out invisibly around me. I
                  hear the slightest crack on the air above the dripping
                  rain and smell the dank dusty rhododendron foliage
                        nearby in awful awareness...
I fight down the anger, the stupidity, the fear, the loneliness that fills
                        me, the space left by the integrity...
Now I am nothing, burned up again by my ridiculous impulses...
I stoop and scratch weakly in the earth by the cooling body and
            feel their eyes boring into me from behind the trees, boring
                  into my back, and feel their hands, their knives, their
                        bludgeoning cudgels bashing out my brains...

•

OK, So I've been put on this planet,
Now I've got to shit and piss
And climb farting up the ladder of success.
I shall never get my mind out of my body
As I thought I could do once upon a time.
I'm right here, trapped in my randy flesh
And at the end of it all I'm going to snuff it
Just like every other sage I ever knew.
No amount of cursing or imagining I'm God
Is going to get me out of this life jacket.

Breaking New Ground

Today I'm breaking out!
I'm doing things I never thought I'd do!
I'm breaking rules I never had the courage to break
That once seemed so difficult to imitate.
The birds whistle more clearly and intensely
The sky looks bluer, the clouds more colourful and sculptured
Every tree is in its place
And my mind, which was worn out and nearing its end
Is bathed in beauty,
And any day now I am going to do something which is going to
    get me out

•

Along the beach
where she walks each day. A thousand
eyes for the slavering sea
and its grey sucking mouth, the sky.
Ears for its infant sound.

Rippling, gently now –
A calm surface of foam.

Rising and falling, a million
little foam-flecked breasts,
filled with volumes of
the deep blue-black. A silent
surface, screaming with want.
Shudders for her mother,
remembering the womb, its
dark warm place

Until Now

Until now
She's been calm…
endlessly
cleaning the towns.
She's seemed
able to cope.
Now
the poison's
grown.
Her immense
seas
begin to heave…

My wish
is to witness Her return
before I die,
to see Her rivers
clear
once more,
to feel Her air
fresh
in my face,
to see vines
grow
through brickwork
and grass
crack
the roads,
to see the white
bones
of Her predators

bleached
by Her light.

The alternative
I fear
is a world
where only
Her pests
survive,
kept back each day
by chemical foams and
fires
invented by the men
to save their skins.
For as he dies
he'll take
Her with him.

We'll be forced
to hide
in modern caves,
fear
the rolling
chlorine
clouds eating
through our shells
closer to our hearts.
Earth will turn
to chemical marsh.
Even her pests
will die.

It's ironic
that mankind's actually
a part of Her,
spawned
in Her lap
and She cannot
tell him
the error of his ways
but lies unspeaking
as he positions
himself
for yet another assault.

The universe
weeps
for its beautiful wife
and pours
avenues
of cold
stars
hatefully
over its son's head.
It *could*
take its son
into the icy vacuum,
and kill him.
But at such a distance
its authority
is scarcely felt.

They tear down the houses
that hold history

in their stare.
They traipse
about the countryside
dropping litter, filling
streams with their garbage,
believing She
has the power
to endlessly
digest their droppings!
They walk across the Earth mocking
sincerity,
setting
as example
cruelty and selfishness.
Innocents die,
unable to hide
their stigma.
The 'weak' grow mad –
or poor –
building mountains
for the ravagers,
festering in gaols
so their enemies
may keep
what they call
their self-righteousness.

Raped,
She lies still,
paler than ever,
soon to release
Her final pleasure.

And there is no mistress
quite like her.
She never gets mean
or miserable.
When she gives Herself
she never gets
possessive
or jealous.
She lets me
leave Her
when I like.
She cleans and
soothes and takes out
the dry cracks.
She hides me
from Their prying eyes
with her rich foliage,
so I can strip off my
clothes and my
civility
for the freedom I need
to escape my race.
She is the most
perfect Woman I know.

Trapped by job and house,
I feel Her air
stab through city haze....
Imprisoned behind windshield,
I see Her light
support clouds between houses....
Sealed by sheets,

I feel Her climb
the stairs to my room....

Like Her tides,
She keeps coming back – but how much more
can she take?

Autumn Poem

I tried to
stop summer going
but now
leaves clog
the paths
and
shiny grey
beech trunks
ghost upwards
into the
frosty air

•

In the morning's All Clear
Eight men came on the deer.
They crouched low on their guns
(Standing, they had the runs).
The day was a long one, as hunts go
Everyone had a bit to throw
Right down from the man in the straw hat with puds on
To the little kid with gloves on.
One deer was hard to get
And had to be bagged by the vet;
It keeled o'er on its ashen haunches
While the other hunters had their lunches.
While they ate they heard the killing shot
Supped their joints and drank their lot,
And when the vet came stumbling back
They shot him after wine.

The morning wore on, that fateful day
And the hunt moved from the grass to the hay.
The golden fields burnt brown by the sun
Were more than the party could stand on the run.
They were taking the bend at the base of the Clear
When they sighted the awful sight of the deer.
The deer had guns and were riding in cars;
They were speeding along, outstripping their Mas.
The huntsmen giggled and ran for cover
But they weren't quick enough
And the cars ran them o'er.
Their bodies were scraped from the burnt brown fields
And whipped red-and-white and given t'seals.

1975–1979

•

All things must have an eye
The eye of the vulcan bomber
The eye of the swallow
The eye of the grasshopper
The eye of infinity

•

my being radiates longing
for the things it never had
my heart overflows with love
it longs to give all it can
but it cannot give
the things it never had

The Mad Girl

The mad girl sits there
Tears trickle down her puffed-up face
The tears of not-knowingness
The tears of a million canes
A smile bends her face when the men rise
They pat her head but they pass on by
The smile tells all about her
It hangs there in the air
A bright line of pain disguised with flickering fur
Deep in her heart she knows what's what
The irons cramp her brain
The bands enclose her body
The hands that put them there are dead
She is alone on the edge of time

The world passes her by
She is powerless to help it
Powerless to stop it
It does not want to stop for *her*
The anguish in her eyes tells all
Why can't she have just a small piece of the world?
Why does the girl with the boy look ten feet tall?
Her womb is barren
No man will put his prick in there
Her mind is withering on the spikes of hate

Mama said a long time ago
Mama said her life was done
She'd have to pass it on the daughter
The perms, the handbags, the tights, the puffs
The leers, the leches, the creepy crawlies
She'd have to give it, with the hands of men...

The dresses fitted her
The hairstyles looked good
The high shoes gave her airs
The rings shone in her ears
She hung out in the bars
She spoke to the men in the know
But the men didn't want to know

The mad girl sits there
Her hair is lax and dull
Wrinkles have grown on her fingers
Her mind fires sparks from its prison
Not-knowingness appears in its tower
It looks down on her sorry condition
The world looked so simple
She did the right things

Her seat is in the dark
It is hidden in shadow
She cannot rise from its grip
The eyes of the others press in
They spit at their naked self in horror
Their looks of horror stain in her mind
But then she realizes *their* fear

From her castle shines a ray of light
A forgotten memory stirs
Once she saw that face of horror
It peered out at her
The face of death in the mirror
A death so sweet and painful
In that moment she glimpsed the lightning truth

That all men and women are afraid of the void
They too are afraid of the stabbing knife
They too fear the treacherous fall of slipping
Their masks sliding from their faces
Their positions caving in beneath them

The wood lets go its grip
Taking heart she rises from her seat
She stumbles to the world clutching at her heart
Her foulness, her obscenities rise in the air
Passersby turn and stare and pass on by
She screams out at their backs for all she's worth
'God never gave you bodies to cover in shit!
'God never gave you balls to make bloody motorcars!
'God never gave you an arse to bung up!
'God take off your plastic smiles!
'God take off your plastic coats!
'God take off your plastic cunts!
'God take it all off, like me!
'I've worked my fingers to the bone!
'I've been moved around for my stench!
'I've had my cunt stitched by your cold stares!
'My body looks fat and raddled and no man has touched it!
'But I'm not taking any more of your shit!
'I'm starting to live whether you like it or not!
'Insult me abuse me and ignore me all you want!
'This time I'll not go away!"

The cars move in
The ambulance men come
The iron spikes inside her begin to vibrate threateningly
The men move towards her

They carry the needles of hate
They fear her presence
The time when she could be left alone has gone
The spikes shake in her flesh
Her ribs snap
She screams as the needles stab-in
Her blood escapes on the pavement
It runs away
Her body sags
It folds like a flower
Her impossible being lies still in their arms
They move it stiffly to the board
They hold up the arm and it flops

The mad girl sits there
Her thoughts are gone
They rise like petals in the sky
They can be touched by no man
The hands that put them there are dead
She is alone
Her invisible tears fall down her absent face
Her invisible smile tells all about her
The universe passes her by
Mama said a long *long* time ago
Mama said her life was done

The Sitting Ducks

The world winds down
The places disappear
Souls rise up from it every day
Some rise above themselves
They see a path they think they ought to take
Some let themselves be taken
They cannot see *that* far beyond the horizon
The true takers though have no direction to take
But sit on the earth like rocks
And wait for the birds to peck out their eyes
Their ghosts rise from the surface of the earth
They go up into space
Where they meet friendly souls like themselves
In space they see the earth decked out with flowers
They see earth covered by cinders and tickertape
They invent games to see who can jaunt the furthest
And eat breakfast and glide about amongst the stars
Eventually they'll come down
But they're not out of energy yet
When they are they'll return to their motionless bodies
They'll sit and wait, watching the antics of their fellows
The followers, the racers, the speedsters, the hipsters, the flipsters
They'll watch the earth's peoples winding down
They'll watch the places disappear

The New Man

Eyes from the past float in the wreckage of the spaceships
Mouths from the future boom our their message of life
In the wreckage the men are trapped
They cannot leave their earthliness behind
Their bodies drift sadly about in the debris
Their minds have never been able to step out
Space pulses – it glows with a strange fire
It bursts outwards like a stupendous flower
The stained glass windows blow outwards
The coloured shards spread out through space
They glint in the light from the sun
Mankind is dead
A new fragile life crawls from the wreckage
It holds up its arms to the golden flower
It strides out
The eyes from the past shrivel and turn to dust
The mouths from the future suck noisily
Their lips swell red, luscious and full
Their throats send out the sound of tinkling bells
The figure walks towards the burst mass of golden light
Her being vibrates with a boundless energy
Flowers and creepers unfurl
Their tendrils fill the space about her
She climbs out along the island of flowers and sits back as earth
    disappears
The stonework of the cathedral crumbles and tumbles
The giant flowers of life bear her away into infinite space

•

you in your smart clothes
your poised mind
your figures of speech
your raised finger
delicately lifted from your glass
your fast car
your amused eye
finding comfort
over a fallen colleague

Love Poem for V

I came back
and found the plates
exactly as I left them

crumbs
the air in the room
all were the same
as they were
on the morning
I left to see you

now the room
seems lived in
worn out
spent
like a dud firework

but you *were* there
on the sea shore
hair blowing in the wind
sun blinding our eyes
lips crushed
on mine

The Cracks in the Neighbourhood

This house
With its gable-end
Done in black
And white timber
On one wing
And its tall
Ground-to-floor chimney
Of fashionable yellow brick
On another,
Must have meant something
To someone
Sometime
Before these provincials
And cosmopolitans
With their sharkskin coats
And their Jenson cars
And their
I M P E R S O N A L I T I E S
Started creeping in.

Ghosts

The Bomb explodes
Because of the emptiness,
The land shrinks
From a fiery breath
And once again
There is only the calm and the quiet of space
Lapping at the Earth
Like a great and timeless sea,
Only a thin and lifeless chill
That blows on the land
As it used to be.

Reason says
That I stand alone,
Listening to this wind,
Comprehending this new wasteland,
But I feel inchoate,
A limb without means.
There can be no person
Such as I
Only the chance
Projections from the past
That bob up and down
On the wind
Too frightened to endure,
No man to appreciate
The futility
Of life lost
After so much
By those who tried to fathom
The hard beauty of the stars...
No other

To walk in admiration
Of man's fleeting majesty,
For the stars are too far.
The flesh will destroy itself
Wherever it springs.
There can now
Only be truth,
A harsh
Unperceived beauty of matter,
Glimpsed yet unglimpsed
During mankind's life,
A glorious peepshow beyond death
To which all men have striven
And at last achieved.

A phantom housewife
Complete with apron,
Brush, and crying child
Appeared before me
Despairingly
In the air.
'I tried to do my best,
And suckle up to my husband
And bring up our son.
It was my husband
Who never played true,
Who made my life an agony
From beginning to end
And took my mind
Off what I really wanted to do –
My real aim in life
Was to be a model,

A glamour girl
Who all men would love,
Who could rule all eternity.
I would have stopped the war
And saved the world from this.'
She fled with
Her struggling child,
Impelled by the wind,
Her form weaker now
And less able to exist,
But her bit had been said
And her last role
Played out to its utmost.

A car worker took her place
His ghostly skin dulled
And listless,
But his eyes aglint
With a final energy.
'I worked fucking hard
Fixing panels to chassis
Day after day
Stinking with sweat
And fouling my lungs
With metal dust.
The noise of the line
Was never out
Of my ears.
The monotony
Drove me mad. I never
Wanted to do
That God-awful job

In the first place,
But with a wife and kids
What can you do
But buckle down?
What I wanted to be was
A player on the pitch.
I was good at rugger,
But after I got married
Somehow there was never the time.
I got more interested
In getting my wage rise
Than watching what was happening.'
The man belched
And farted
And he too began fading,
Joining the spore of particles
Left behind by the woman.

A novelist appeared next,
His hair long and wild,
His body tall and lean,
Still with the clothes he wore
On the day he died.
He opened both his arms
In a gesture of despair
And shook his head.
'Of course I saw it all coming.
I warned the world in advance
But no one listened.
During my life I achieved what I wanted to,
One of the lucky ones I suppose,
But only at great expense

To my family and others.
Nevertheless I was able
To tour the world
Having a quiet word
In everyone's ear,
And I put in my bit
To save you all.'
Still shaking his head
But looking faintly happy now
He was carried away
On the wind, papers
Streaming from his arms,
The useless efforts
Of his life's work.

A farmer pulled-up
In the cab of his tractor,
Its engine shimmering
And roaring, as though real.
His lips were pursed
In tight amusement,
But his head was sunk with restrained anger
And his eyes stared frozenly from their sockets.
'I too knew what was going on.
How could I ignore it
When my fields were withering
From insecticides
And my soils turning
To fertiliser dust?
My animals were cruelly treated
To make ends meet.
I was forced into a position

In which I never wanted to find myself.
What I wanted was
To be at one
With the Earth,
To enrichen its soil
Not to strip it,
But the pigs
In the cities,
The hungry bastards,
Ate everything
Faster that I could produce it
And still wanted more.
In the end I took my kerosene
To the cities to burn them down,
But by then it was too late.'
He shook his fists at the sand clouds
In a sudden last expression
Of his reasonable body,
Then he turned back to his controls
And revved quickly away,
Depriving the wind of its part.

An economist appeared,
Laughing loudly
And shaking all over
With his nerves.
He wore a suit
And a gold clock
Strapped to his wrist
That he consulted
To keep informed
Of elapsed time.

'Ha! You *would*
Like to blame me!
But I can tell you
With all honesty
I knew nothing!
My system was sound
And my advice given in good faith.
I practiced all my life
To make sure that I became
A man of the world
Before giving you my secrets.
I always wanted to be
What I was.
I loved my job
And I'm sorry now
That we can't all be around
To continue…'
A silken scarf
Which he had been
Carrying to wipe his brow
Fluttered by him in the wind
And gagged on his mouth,
Muffling the final words
He wanted to say.

An industrialist
Trod the empty spot
Looking warily about him
As he spoke.
'I never wanted to be an industrialist.
I wanted to be a poet
And soar on high

Taking the whole human race
With me. But
I was no good with words
And the words I did produce
Never gave me a proper income.
I was forced to prostitute
What little talent I possessed
And go into the Business.
I was unhappy, and lonely,
But as I rose higher
I eventually began to
Reach the limits I had set myself
As a poet, and for a while
I grew happy with my lot.
But instead of elevating
My fellow men
I left them
Blind and purposeless,
And I must confess
That it might have been I
Who conferred with colleagues
And international governments
And unwittingly created
The conditions that
Have led to this.'
Frightened and cowed
His visage was torn apart
By a sudden, unexplained
Fury in the wind
And his ghostly fragments
Were spun away
Into space.

A politician
Reluctantly
Appeared,
Smiling and then frowning,
At first speechless,
And dressless, his words
Finding no sure direction,
His clothes no occasion,
But eventually he spoke, and
As he did, the Earth trembled
And shook. Gaping cracks
Appeared in the desert.
Mountains tumbled down
Behind him, and when he
Had finished his brilliant oratory
Applause soared from behind the sky
In a continuous, beating thunder
That echoed round
The globe, sounding his curtain.
Then the cleansing wind
Gathered his protesting form
On its way.

Next came a holy man – a priest, an imam, a
Rabbi,
Smoothing down
His apparel, and holding up
A single finger
To command attention
From the whistling sand.
'It was I
Who conferred with brothers

And believers
Around the world
In our grief and anger
Who brought down Gomorrah.
In the Bible, the Torah,
The Koran
Was it not said that
Jesus, the Messiah, Mohammad
Will reign again?'

And finally, in the debris,
A virgin ballerina appeared,
Her sure, white legs extended
And her graceful arms
Curved above her arched spine.
She trilled on her toes
Before gracefully launching herself
Across the sand,
Her ghost the last
And most difficult to depart
As she carried all men and women,
All ages
And all promise of the future,
Away,
In her movement.

There can be no plea
For vanity,
Only pale, mental residues,
Shadows of a former life.
And only these ghosts,
The striven memories of men,

Can find a purpose in the wind,
Carried around the globe
In storms of dust,
Chattering and arguing
About the rights and wrongs –
The echoes of a past
That will never finally fade
But will always travel outwards through space
Long after the Earth herself
Has crumbled
And the stars
Have rearranged.

In the Modern World

Technique
is first
out of
the window,
demanding
commitment
that cannot
be mustered.
It is replaced
by cleverness.
Purpose
is replaced
by righteousness.
Experience
by a manageable
ignorance.

•

the
clock
ticking
like a bomb
beside
my
bed

The Union

When evening comes
We organise the union.
Across the beer tables where we laugh and groan
All we wish for is the deliverance of our sins
So that we may wallow in the ancient troughs of pleasure
Which are ours by birth
And procreate happily under the sun.
This ale is what we swear by.
These one-armed bandits are what we play by.
And when our work is done at the end of the day
This place is where we come
And in here we find an infinite union of our souls
An infinite union of our thoughts
Stretching into the evening of our lives,
But when the closing doors arrive
And we stagger out
Under the impersonal glare of the lamps
We are hard put to avoid the swerving cars
And have to face the humiliation of arriving home,
Unchallenged and unchallengeable,
And lose ourselves in the misery of sleep
And wake on yet another day of cold and clashing signs.

•

I can remember
when she gave me
my first big kick.
I felt weak and tired
from the demands of life
and the pace I had to keep
just to stay alive.
As I hurried
through the sprawl of buildings
an uncanny sickness
fell on me
like a grey cloak
that would not go away
but grew heavier
as time passed.

Feeling that death was near,
I entered the beauty
of a cleansing wood.
Startled by her presence
I walked slowly
in a trance
as though seeing her
for the last time.
She presented a
succession of
magical scenes…
pathways
that disappeared, fallen
boughs apple-green and
damp with moss… every
step took me

to a sight
more breathtaking
than the last,
all illuminated by
her light which
bathed everywhere.

Her rays sliced
through the
tree-top canopies
above my head
splintering, breaking
into a million crystal jewels
on her leaves,
the glinting
lights
standing bravely
erect
like
candles at my
coffin's side.
The bushy arms
of the rhododendrons
spilled down
at my feet
laden with untidy
pink flowers
and radiant
with dim light.

At death's side, impulsively
I stripped off.

The distant world
at large
receded
like an
unlovely star
of poisoned air
and barbarous
inhabitants.
More important
to me now
were the tiny black
insects
that crawled
from flower to flower,
the wholesome smell of
her,
the forest
growths and
her aged floor
thick
with countless years
of decay.

Light,
furry creatures
ran claw-
footed up
her twisting barks,
and everywhere
were eyes,
touching my flesh
with abusive thoughts,

repaying me.
Yet their owners were
getting off too,
and with this thought
I rose, and
moved heavily through
her cool leaves,
and felt
her cool air
on my skin,
nourished
by the freedom
I felt
to play naked as
a child,
run
flowers along my arms and
bite
her gently
with my teeth.

Her lush
vegetation
weighed heavily against
me, like the walls
of a tomb.
The flowers became
Intense, vivid
urging me on.
My prick
heavy,
erect,

bludgeoned
into her soft
green leaves.
The dull pain
of its root
ached.
My hands worked,
paying close attention,
while the greedy
eyes
caressed
where
I fell
sensitised
to their touch.

Yet still I felt
an even more urgent
need
to give myself to
her
more fully.
Crude,
fleshy conditions
begged
to be prepared.
Behind
the radiant faces
of the flowers were
hard twigs
and suddenly I
longed to

feel their cruelty.
Roughly,
I broke
a stem
from one of
her precious leaves,
and watched the green
sap oozing from the gash,
and eased the flayed
end
gently inside me.

Impaled,
foolishly-postured,
uncaring
before her presence
my hands worked on,
one pressing
the swollen glans, the
other moving
the stem in
its fleshy holder,
scratching the walls.
Anguishedly,
I beat my head
against the ground
in pleasure
in pain.
There seemed
no possible
way
to express

the fullest extent
of my feelings
for her
whom I so sweetly loved.

The Chemical Genesis of the Known Universe

On the first day
The cyclohexylaminic dawn
Broke over the chloral anhydrones
Of the dipentane landscapes
In the ionones
And the upper ketones

On the second day
The furfuryl monster
In the allantoin exhibition,
And the formamide creature,
Were all butyraldehyding

On the third day
The clepta-hecta-gamma-butyrolacetone,
The crotonic aldehyde,
The nicotinamide,
The valeric nightmare,
The diethyl nettle,
The 1,2-epoxy bromo-stricta-palmitate creature
And theta aniline
Had all been formed

The bromo phenyls,
The cupric dekalin
And the tri-chloro-terpin reagent for the annihilation of anisics
Formed the resorcinol lactate
Which settled out on the fourth day

From this came the greater succinates
And all the chemical nightmares –
The nitric esters

And tetryl ethers
That precipitated on the fifth day

On the sixth day
The dicyclo oxalone galaxy was formed

On the seventh
There was industrial unrest among the technical staff

•

unscalable rock faces
rising from the ocean's depth
and topped with secret paths
winding through gorse and bracken
below a pale misty sky –
the mingled fancies of my youth

beneath the craggy cliffs
huddled with crofts
a beach strewn with the wild sea's litter,
sea-weed and tarred pebble,
tin can and white porous bone....
A scene I saw, once,
in my dream of childhood.

1979–1989

The 1980s – Part One

I GET UP
I GO TO WORK
THE CLOCK GOES ROUND
I GET UP
I GO TO WORK
THE CLOCK GOES ROUND
I GET UP
I GO TO WORK
THE CLOCK GOES ROUND
I GET UP
I GO TO WORK
THE CLOCK GOES ROUND
I GET UP
I GO TO WORK
THE CLOCK GOES ROUND
I GET UP
I GO TO WORK
THE CLOCK GOES ROUND
I GET UP
I GO TO WORK
THE CLOCK GOES ROUND
I GET UP
I GO TO WORK
THE CLOCK GOES ROUND
I GET UP

The 1980s – Part Two

THE PAIN OF LIFE
THE CLOCK
THE PAIN OF LIFE
THE COCK
THE PAIN OF LIFE
THE CLOCK
THE PAIN OF LIFE
THE COCK
THE PAIN OF LIFE
THE CLOCK
THE PAIN OF LIFE
THE COCK
THE PAIN OF LIFE
THE CLOCK
THE PAIN OF LIFE
THE COCK
THE PAIN OF LIFE
THE CLOCK
THE PAIN OF LIFE
THE COCK
THE PAIN OF LIFE
THE CLOCK

•

I lie in bed
Surfeit and dead
My bones are hard
My skin is lard
My eyes have fed
My brain has bled

My arms are crossed
My soul is lost
My bed is dust
The ground is lust
And life has washed
And got me sloshed

I've had too much
Of such and such
Too much lying
Too much crying
I've been a butch
And used a crutch

Now fly me up
I'll take my sup
If there's a hell
Or a high bell
In your sour cup
And be your pup

●

From time to time the world reminds
The old man of his past and binds
Him to a life he'd thought had gone –
The world when everything was one.

Before the war had been a calm
A certain peace now never seen
A certainty that life was there
And not a mishmash in the air.

There had been fewer cares to bear
And less rush, and less to wear,
One tradition of which to think
And not the modern kitchen sink.

The scenes that draw him back in time
And those that straggle out of line
A lone forgotten country house,
A smile, or favour – one of those.

●

Me a society visitor,
Don't like to stay.
Get what I want
Then go my way.
Each place I stop off at
Gets me a little higher,
Until I get off at
The top
Like a flower.

Juxtapositions

1.
Our ships will rise – tall spires of knowledge
Into the black.
Bright orbs will circle Earth,
Platforms for our endeavours.

My space seed
Rooted in earth
Trails forlornly as we fly
Stretched thin out of love.

2.
The cities of the future
Will look like the cities of now.
Busloads of commuters
Will travel endlessly back and forth
Back and forth
In smoke-filled compartments
Through ghettoed estates.

Money will run out.

Who says we will grow more generous?

On the contrary we will grow more hateful, and smaller.

3.
Man, beautiful Man.
Your head broken by your dreams.
Why are you so foolish that you attempt the impossible?

4.

The Devil is flesh from which we cannot separate the spirit.

5.

The soul has no right to sit in judgment of a dead earth.

6.

There is no answer to the black face of destitution.

Frightened of the load,
Man after woman,
You sink like skittles.

7.

We fly like winged immortals
Raging through the storm.
Our hearts batter
At dead casks
Made tough by repeated drowning.
We sleep in poisoned rags
Thrown around us by desire.
We wait for the morrow
With burning breaths that flicker
And die in the night.

Love is no more than desperation.
Small children are curses that further our end.
We make scratches at the undersides of life.
And the fuel that leaks from our tails
As we rise away
Leaves a scourging ball of fire that
Obliterates all we have built.

The 1980s – Part Three

Brutal mothers
Slash young son's wrists.
Gays are beaten to pulp.
Smiling bowler-hatted gents
lose their teeth
in underground toilets.
Fathers
decapitate their daughters.
Crane jibs
swing across streets
slicing through masonry
and tip boiling lead into screaming crowds.
Murderers stalk alleyways
in broad daylight
ripping shoppers' hearts.
Children with guns
and black hangman's hoods
stand at bank corners
waving-in the frightened guards.
Brother fucks sister,
then strangles her.
A mother rips open the chest
of her 4-year-old,
and hungrily sucks up the blood;
her face, disgorged,
drips crimson as it pans round
the nervous crowd
with an accusing glare.
Gangs of East End garage mechanics
and scrap dealers
break in and attack families round their TVs, as
dwarves and midgets swarm in the parks

uprooting shrubs and destroying flower beds,
and inside primary school canteens
junk-eating children
hack teachers to death.

Three Poems

1.

Silent black forms
Curl in the night, and
I wake on visions
Of My Girl
(The one I could have had)
In her plush suburbia home
Happy now that she's
Got her two-bit wager
To sugar her muff
And suck his lot
At the television set

2.

I sit in endless
Misery, sampling the
Harsh brightness
Of the stars.
They are so pure
And far –
We are so feeble
And thin! –
And always I think
What chance can there be
For beetles like us
That crawl through the years
On our backs of jet
Struggling
With our love?

3.
There is no escape
For the celestial concubine
Who fucks the stars
And leaves the Earth unkill'd
Who must pass his time
In fancies of the night
Waking enviously
On the dead
Who dance with inward eye

Wanker

Time for a wank. I always
Wank myself out at the end of the day.
I get into my bed – which
Is like a little rat's hole, warm
And Secure and
Away from people –
And wank.

History lesson

The power of man
The power of God
The power of Kings
The power of people
The power of man

•

When I was asked by Mary Lou
I gave her my shoe
I gave her my glue
I gave her my stew
I gave her all my blue
What about you?
What about you?
Did you give her your shoe?
Did you give her your glue?
Did you give her your stew?
Did you give her all of your blue?
Did you? Did You?
Did you *fuck*, you!
You milked her breast!
You stole her vest
You sent her West!
You took her *zest!*

The Ogi Men

With trembling, gill-like fronds
THE OGI MEN
Felt through my flimsy wall
And reduced my room
To a pile of smoking ash
Whilst round the TV
My family sat
Watching baked beans
Pour in
T R E M B L I N G streams
From the tin

The Ogi Men
Have tried to reach me
All this while
And in my fear
I have been unable to hear
Their nightly voices
Call me through the air
But now they have got me
I have no recourse
But to be led by their fronds
Down the stairs
While my family sit
In their chairs

But where will we go?
Back to their ships
That wait
Near the bins
Where the chip eaters
Hang out with their mates?

Or further in
To the watery bowels
Of the house
Where Ogi Men die
Holding their heads
With their voluble mouths
Their lips so big
If they flapped
They would fly?

We go instead
To the Cumpen Moars
That have risen their backs
In the attic
To attract the flies
Which they eat
While they boil their feet
In the steam from the kitchen
That floats up the stairs
And condenses in droplets
On bed-stead legs
And the arms of old chairs,
Where I bump into junk
And last year's boxes of shirts
And slip on my marbles
And where the Ogi Men
Finally crackle their fronds
AND TAKE ME AWAY

Space Radio

Space Radio… Space Radio…

Space Radio… Space Radio…

This is the *last* Space Radio broadcast.

We cannot reach you with our words
Because of the way you behave,
Because of the way you trip your feet
And snap your fingers
To an inner symphony we cannot hear,
Therefore, we must leave you to your fate.

This is the *last* Space Radio broadcast.

We have tried to reach you
Through your schools
Through your journals,
Your television, your art shows;
We have tried through your governments,
Through your cinema and your town planning;
We have even tried through your plumbing,
Your ten-pin bowling.
We have written novels
And published millions of books
In a language that attracts your eye;
We have altered the courses of rivers
And put warnings in the lines of airplane designs;
We have tried to reach you through the sweets you suck;
The videos you listen to;
Through your partners' roll-on deodourants
Or the flavour of your tea;

Through the kind of glue you sniff,
Or the kind of rock'n'roll music you listen to,
Or the brand of cigarette you smoke...
But it has all been in vain.
You have thought it all a mirage,
A con trick, or a game.

This is the *last* Space Radio broadcast.

Space Radio was launched secretly
By a consortium of artists and free men
In July, Nineteen Sixty Three,
When the dangers of overpopulation
And the possibility of nuclear war
And death by pollution, and urban decay,
Had become an hourly anxiety of our race,
And forced us to take our drastic action.
It was on the day when the stars became a human frontier
With the launch into space of our hero, Yuri Gagarin.

Since then, repeated broadcasts have been made to you
By us, your artists and writers
To warn you of the perils you face.
But now, after long trials
And the exhaustion of our fuel
And the bankruptcy of our souls
We have been forced to concede defeat.

This has been the *last* Space Radio broadcast.

And now... the curtain drawn once more
You may *continue* with your entertainment.

the snammer-man

in God's backyard
a blue-throated
bull-roaring
snammer-man
lay down to die,
its marled eyes shot
with quinces and golds
from the glorious sights
it had seen
in the airs of its life
above where the drain pipe
guttered its filth,
and in its arms
was caught
a soft-breathing
snammer-girl
who had finally come
from the Tropics of Daz
to lend it her mind
in the tumult
of its last
fleeting hours

In Dunham Park

On a day like this
Even Crow
Looks elegant
As she launches herself
Across the void
Hardly moving
Suspended by anti-grav.
Her great ragged wings
Raise themselves
And beat
Once

•

        The end will arrive
        Like the bailiffs.

•

When all the charging about's been done
And 'inanimate' matter's rearranged.

•

        This voice, recognisable
        To a few good friends
        Is going out fast.
        Hurry up. Tell me
        What I don't know,
        Is it past?

A weight of fog, please

Tongue-tied, dense,
Fumbling for words-that-will-do –
Being misinterpreted,
Acquiring lucidity at
Odd moments,
When my thoughts are no use
To anyone but me.

O fleet rare window, you
Desert me still. This line or two
Was meant to pin you down. It
Is not exactly an ode to you.

Bus Stop

Standing in line
To the call of Time.

Feelin' kind'a blue

A bitter son crept from his dad's bed,
Stole downstairs,
Got into his dad's car
And took a ride
To see what he could see.

But the car ran out of juice,
No way back and no way on.
There ain't no kid tried harder than me.

•

Dark world
I can write about you
In reams,
But what use is it
When what I've done
Has somehow slipped the mark?

I'm a poet
A prose writer by default,
So the form is pretty odd
But this shouldn't
Fox you

Energy leaks
As eagerly as blood
From an exposed vein.
I can't keep
Re-writing
What I've already well said.

•

Moral of the dark night –
NOT to give up!

Slow, soulful jazz song

This is the first day
Of the new calendar
The one I told you about
On our first kiss
This is the new day
Of the whole year
We'll be in love

I told you
When I met you
There would be
No tomorrow
But what I meant was
There'd be several

I had my
Golden armour on
To protect me
But what I meant was
Hold on to me

This is the first day
Of the new calendar
When you said you'd
Go with me
This is the new life
We said we'd live

You slipped by
In my dreams
And I cried
When I saw you'd gone.

Be my lover –
Please.

I can feel
In my heart
It'll be okay
To hold back the clock
If only
You would too

This is the first day
Of the new calendar
The one in space
They call the 'step'
For mankind

How can I
Forget you,
Don't resist
This is the time
To fall in love

This is the first day
Of the new calendar
The one I told you about
On our first kiss
This is the new day
Of the whole year
We'll be in love

(Composed at Nick Turner's Cadillac Ranch)

Michael Butterworth

I'm clinging to the rock face

How long will it be until the next time
I feel a timeless moment
On the long drop?

1989—2001

•

These strange things called trees
Like missiles thudding
Nose-down in the earth
Stuck unwavering like thrown knives,
Or darts, their alveoli flights
Sprayed like twisted limbs
In intricate array.
Inevitably, like the rest of Nature
They will succumb
To a grim determination.
In their museums
They will look even stranger

Mouselow

When the wind blows from the hill
You jump the gun and say, "God, I'm ready to go now."
But then you feel the softness of that same wind,
"Oh no, Christ, sorry, not yet."

at pant-yr-esgair

hills like silver
backed whales

For Sophie and Lianne

Bibble
Bobble
Babble
Here
Comes
Mr
Hubble
Watch him bibble
Watch him bobble
Watch him babble
Watch him bubble
Bibble
Bobble
Babble
Bubble

•

The punctual face of the blind ripper appeared in my mirror one
    day as I shaved.
This is the face of a man who is quartered by Time, I said to myself,
He has woken to find the worlds of dream singeing his brow.

Two Poems

1.
I have decided to wear
My underpants
Over my trousers
In Day-Glo lemon –
On bright evenings on
Autumnal days
When the giggling
Of the office girls
Is more bearable.

At other times
I claim the right
To wear them on my head;
But then they must be
Bright gold –
And I mustn't walk
Cross-footed.

2.
I shall wind down
Many days
Of my life
Before I am done;
I shall ask the Christ
For absolution,
And bury my bones
In a small wood
Overlooking Bottoms.
It is just near
Where the pylons
March up and down.

For Charlotte

A merman on the sea
Gently cries his name
And the names of those who
Cross his wat'ry main…

A paean for all their woes had he
And for the fishes too
To make the hearts that travel free
Be especially true!

So, mermaids of the sea
Let your heartstrings fly
When travel you there
'cross such proment'ry!

For Martin

Martin, you were such a handsome guy
The way your features were arranged,
But maybe how they are now
Is how you wanted them?
We weren't judgemental
You liked us because of this
And I won't let you down now.
But, lover,
It's gonna take a long time

This one,
To put ourselves back together again
And walk away.

(For Savoy Books' anti-publicity manager, who 'jumped the ether'.)

Michael Butterworth

Zazen at Bookchain

All day sitting
Selling shrink-wrap
Drinking juice
And not a bailiff in sight

Ode to no One in Particular

I will carve your face
With broken hieroglyphics
To get at your
China roots
If my boat doesn't land

For Natalia

Nat the bat
Ate a cat
Saw a rat
(Tittle-tat)
Went adroit
Around the flat
To find a mat
To sick the cat
To catch the rat
(Rat-a-tat)
She found a DAT
And then begat
A tuneful brat
And that was that
(Nice'n'pat)!

Signed: A Twat

For Lucy

If a pea
Is not a pea
When it is a flea,
Is a flea
Not a pea
When it is pea?

For S

Sweet   Little   Pea
What'you going to do to me?
Can I wake you up to see?
Sweet
        Little
               Pea

The Storehouse of life

Once strong and mysterious,
Now words come slow and hard,
They tumble from locked garrets
And swiftly flee

2001—2020

Love poem for S

To my Darling
Buddha Bee!
The words of love you gave to me from your heart
By the stream or
Silver wood
Stirred in me the strong feelings of love I have for you,
And through these spring flowers
Dancing in the wind
I return it to you.

For Richard Kostelanetz

P A
M P R T

G O
B D G T

U
B
B D G M N P R S T

D U
B C   D G N P

Y A
K   M P W Y

W O
N P T W

T O
D G N P   R T W

I ran out of time

At Ladybarn

In warm gusts
Staccato drops
Plash against
The glass

They beat harder
With an urgent
Velocity

I don't know when – maybe some
Fifteen years ago
We were often
Awoken gently
By Roberto
Practising his piano,
Or Squirrel Nutkin
Racing through the eaves
Above our heads
To make her nest
Among our books

Reynard the Fox
Played beneath
The cherry trees
Leaving
Scavenged bones
And brightly coloured packets
Trailblazed
Across the lawn

Off to the Riots!

Young boys
Almost men
Ambled below us,
Tubby
At the back
Struggling to keep up.
They could have been
Going to the fair, walking
With the half-purposeful
Casual air of lads
Out on the town,
Except they walked in silence
Listening to their own tread.

Where am I? Here I am!
Summer Poems (After Ryōkan)

Here I am
On the bus
With my suitcase
On another
Adventure.

On the train
To Macclesfield.
Will someone
Claim their seat
From me?
The
Moving
Indicators
Are confusing.

At Caffé Nero
Having coffee
Looking out
Over the square.

◆

Here I am
Waiting for the bus
Watching the traffic.
When will it come?

◆

Here I am
Walking.
Enjoy!
I can't get there
Any faster!

♦

Here I am
Lying in bed.
What will happen
If I don't get up?

Getting ready
To rise from my bath,
Drying my hands
To write this poem.
What will I write?

Rising
To my knees
To wash my face and hair.
Standing
To rinse-off
With the hand-shower,
Shivering.

Here I am
Cooking breakfast.
The eye is always
Ahead of the hand.

What
Can go wrong?

♦

Here I am
Lying in bed
Trying to sleep.
It's so hot.
The moon is a yellow
Children's
Playpiece
In the sky.
Knowing I have a train
To catch tomorrow.

♦

Here I am
At the British Library
Having tea in the sun.
It is much
More pleasant here
Than Euston
Waiting
For my train.

♦

Walking along
In my skin.
What am I worried about?

♦

Here I am
On my own.
S has gone to
Tiratanaloka,
The land of
The Three Jewels!

Here I am
Lying in bed.
I close my eyes.
There are two
Of me,
Very young.
I made a
Pact with death.
One of me
Comes into the house
And plays. The
Other
Knows what happened.

I try to sleep
But anxious thoughts
Keep me awake.
The low thud
Of dance music
From a neighbour's flat.

My room is pale
And white

From my
Bedside lamp.
Traffic noise
And voices
Come and go.
In the warm night
The hours
Come and go.
I wonder
Whether to
Make something to eat?

♦

Here I am
Taking
A month's
Recycling
To the underground
Car park.
Will the cooking
Be spoiled
When I return?
How about
The mobile phone
I've left
Behind by the cooker?
Will someone
Ring me?

Lying here
I will say my last,

If I can speak.
If I can't
I will ride away with you,
Silently.

I will ride away with you, death.
How will I face you
When
You close in on me?

♦

Standing with myself
At the bus stop.
The sun is shining again
After the heavy rain.
Leaving work for home.

♦

I can't believe
It's over.
It's been so lovely!
It's been such fun!

♦

Here we are
Outside Peterborough
On our way to see Paddy
And Inge,

Waiting
For a platform.

◆

Here I am
With you
In the silence
Of the bedroom
Hearing only
The throb of an
Extractor fan
To send us
Off to sleep.

◆

Travelling home
On the 142.
Will I be able
To sit with myself
For that long?

Finding its way
Through the traffic
An ambulance,
Its blue light flashing,
Its siren rising
And falling.

Buddhafield

Here I am,
Dropped like a stone!

The tents
Spring together
Like colourful
Landing craft

The children
Blow bubbles,
Giant
Unstable globes
That flex
In the air
Before crashing

In four days
The pop-up world
Is complete

Buddhafield,
Always renewing herself!

♦

(The Sangha)

Padma D
With a shoulder bag
Of flowers
And a sun scarf
Round her head

Debbie, in a
Summer dress
And a straw hat

Bare-chested
In the sun
Casper dribbles
A football

Natasha and Maya,
Buddhafield's
Resident Cerberus,
Sponsored to keep
Silent for 24hrs
Race by. They
Are on a Harry
Potter mission.

David,
Lying down
In the grass
Surveys us
Through
Dark shades

Sara
Rests in her
Coffee den
In our Camper van

Jenny,
Wears a peaked cap

And ponytail.
She swings a
Sweeping brush
And shouts a
Friendly halloo

Kent
Swings a plastic
Water bottle

In the field
Farmer Mike
Turns his hay

Gem,
Long-trousered
Swings his arms

Hitching her combats,
Annie brushes
Her hair

Uddyotani
Swings a rust-coloured
Towel
And a toothbrush

Chrissie
Shakes a rattle

Robin
Swings a stripy

Bucket, and
Snaps a hill
With his camera

Carl sleeps under the tree
Where the dove sits
On her nest

Dayavajra
Swings a
Straw hat

Hannah
Swings herself

Richard
Has an aria
About him

Dan swings
A blue
'Bench' shirt

Dayaka
Swings a shirt
And a water bottle

Helen swings by
With a
Brightly coloured
Shower towel

Ashleigh
Wears a feather
In her straw hat,
And shades

Vidyabahdri
Wears a stetson
And swings a flask
And a loom band

Cathy
Swings a
'Lifetime'
Shopping bag

Deep in conversation
With Gaia
Eleanor
Carries papers
And bowls

Jane
Carries a towel
And a shower
Bag, slowly
Up the hill

 "Just in case,
I'm going to Velcro it."

Voices
Come and go

On the
Afternoon air

The old
Picket gate
By the barn,
Crowded
With aniseed

♦

With apologies to
Ratnasagara,
Hasavajra, Sangha-
ketu, Tejapushpa
And many
Who did not walk past my chair
Outside my tent
That sunny day

Buddhafield again

The bright
Berries of the
Rowan. The
Young birch
Standing guard.
The white
Poplar
Flashing
At me.
A Cabbage White
Flutters by.
Dragon-flies
Criss-cross
The field.
Sara makes coffee
On the
Campingaz
Camping Chef!
Debbie and Chrissie
And little
Molly
Sit on the
Compost loo

It doesn't
Take long
After the first
Conch blow
For the lunch
Queue to form!

A pool
Fringed with reeds,
At its centre
An island
Made of rocks and trees.
Island Earth

Travelling to meet S

Sunlight
Bounces off
Rainwater
Ripples across the ceiling
While we wait
For drivers to change

A pain
Sits
Waiting to burst
On the edge
Of my heart

•

Gallant?
For fighting?
'The War to End All Wars'?
I can really only
Feel
An angry laugh.

Have you already forgotten
What
Setting loose
The hounds
Of everlasting night
Will do?

Our potential
Pitiably
Stunted
Reduced
Once more
To a wilful
Low
Denominator.

Much Drinking and Little Thinking

Much Drinking
And Little Thinking
Always end up drunk,
Even though both try
Very hard
To stay on the wagon.
Much Drinking will be okay
Until Little Thinking forgets
And buys a can,
Then Much Drinking
Will have one too.
Little Thinking will sober up
But after one can
Much Drinking
Will be unable to stop,
And Little Thinking
Will have another.
In this way
They pass the day.

•

If
Nothing new
Can be said
Then let's not say
Art is dead
Or follow
Any creed
Just describe the
Moment

•

I'm here.
I'm still here.

Reading the Dermot Healey Obit

The bugger, juicing himself like that.
Born November, just a baby!
It's not like the geyser was
Ancient, or summink,
Is it?
Never read him. He seems just like a
Fantastic old bugger, really.
Couldn't he see that
The world was eating his hat?
I'll make recompense
But it's hard to see
People my age
Dying off like this.

•

Plug-in with Sony
Or Apple – and start a war!
Find a universal
Plug – and quick!

•

While our parents live
Life remains
A mystery, and
When they die
There's nothing
Left to know anyway

1958

Arrayed
On the school lawn,
Smiling for the camera

•

Adam was
Made
From Eve.
That
It
Was
The other
Way
Round
Is a
Lie
Told
By a male
Warrior class

On the closing of a local haunt

Drip
Drip
Drip
There was a café
Called Drip
Until
One day
It dripped away

From a train window

All looks
Flat and washed,
Pools of dark mercury
Float
In the fading light.
Blackened trees
Etch their forms
Against the
Flat sky.
So many winters.

They shoot people, don't they?

The old guard
Is fighting back,
In Syria,
In South America,
In Russia,
Soon
Everywhere.
The planet-grabbers,
The fundamentalist
Are the biggest
Shootists
Of them all.

After the Election

In the echoing streets
A car without a silencer
Dopplers into muteness.

Quiet voices
Murmur from
Adjacent balconies

Pain

I hold you in my arms.
We dance around.
Like good partners should
You stand aside
And when I sit you down with me,
Joined together
We are invincible.

•

He remembered
Cradling each other
As the sky burst
With light, then
They ran
To the boathouse,
Where each took a boat,
The night very still
And warm
And eternal.
But she fell
And couldn't get up,
Her hair was
Already loose,
Her skin pallid
And her heart
Thumped away.
She looked up
And the lines in their faces
Fell away
And they smiled
And he closed her eyes
And laid her in the boat
And dragged it
Into the water.

•

Absorbed in work, I forget
You are not here.
Then I have to tell myself
You are not really here,
And this reminds me.

Emptiness

```
THERE IS   TIME
THERE  IS   NO TIME
THERE   IS   TIME
THERE    IS   NO TIME
THERE     IS   TIME
THERE      IS   NO TIME
THERE      IS   TIME
THERE       IS   NO TIME
THERE        IS   TIME
THERE         IS   NO TIME
THERE          IS   TIME
THERE           IS   NO TIME
THERE            IS   TIME
THERE             IS   NO TIME
THERE              IS   TIME
THERE               IS   NO TIME
THERE                IS   TIME
THERE                 IS   NO TIME
THERE                  IS   TIME
THERE                   IS   NO TIME
THERE                    IS   TIME
THERE                     IS   NO TIME
THERE                      IS   TIME
THERE                       IS   NO TIME
THERE                        IS   TIME
THERE                         IS   NO TIME
THERE                          IS   TIME
THERE                           IS   NO TIME
```

Beech Croft Farm

This life
All that is here,
The people,
The red car
A red dot
Moving
Above Wharfdale,
Sara
Lying asleep
Behind me,
This camping chair
And gas bottle
By my side,
The sheep
Calling to
One another, "I am
Here, Here I am,
Over here…
Still here",
Geese
Squabbling,
Poppy and Seal
Running through
The grass,
Hover flies,
The guitarist
Strumming
Quietly outside
His tent.

Later,
Erecting the Relum,

The lowering sun
Casts long shadows,
And a child cries

•

My heart
And head were
Linked
By causeways
Of ink –
It used to be
So simple
To reach you

•

Your eyes wide
Catch mine.
Now we can only look,
But it is enough.

•

I did
The 3-D
Puzzle.
You looked
At me
Amazed,
We
Went for a meal.
You paid.

Early blackbird at Ty Mawr

A lone voice
Cries down
The night

Death of a great mammal

We were given
Advance warning
Years ago:
'There is no such thing
As society.'
Farewell, then,
The Welfare State and the NHS.

Shell Island (Looking out to Bardsey)

The snide laughter
Of gulls
Rain clouds walking
Bandy-legged
Elizabeth and Jenny
In straw hats, and
Wind…

Wind
As waves
As clouds
As sound
As seed heads

Beware Perfidious Albion

On Leaving You, Friendly Europe,
Turning Grande-Bretagne into a low-
tax, small-state, free-trade
nation who will benefit?

Of course,
Ready for war again.

Room

1.
Traffic swells
And ebbs
Through the open
Balcony door
Voices arrive
And join each other
And disappear.
A street cleaner
Whines
And Deliveroo bikes
With
Chopped-
Off
Mufflers
Come and go
Servicing
The dealers
And thieves.

2.
The LED ceiling
Lights gleam
Like six studs

3.
Winky
And Micky
And Sylvester the Cat,
Little Red
And Bunny
And Mrs Bunny,

And Mousey and
Winky Too
Sit on boxes
Above the shrine.
Winky is
Almost as old
As his owner
And has been
Loved and stroked so much
Like the Velveteen Rabbit
His hair
Has gone

4.
The warm
Night air
Breathes
Into the room
And a carpet moth
Flies erratically
Across the vast space

•

Here I am
Sitting in my skin
At seventy.
Happy Christmas,
Dude.

Three connected poems

Noting the appearance
Each year
Of the sweet-
Smelling furze
I began my voyage.

I used to think
I had
A sea to cross.
Of course,
I was there
All the time.

Signs may
Speed death along, but
Being formless
There is no death
To speed to.

The Playground

When I
Gave up the
Front seat
To another
It was
To please them.
Now, at
The end
It is the same.
I will take
The front seat.

The Racist English

If you're black
You're going back.
(The Home Office)

"When you try black
There's no going back."
(Nicholas Van Hoogstraten)

Cooperation

If anything's
Gonna save the world
It's got two 'Os'.

●

The fastest
Spreading thing
In the world
Is a smile

●

You can have me. But
I am going to get
Very, very
BIG

Two Poems

Memories
Join together
Like guests
Arriving at a party.
Perhaps they
Always have.
But once
They came so fast,
I mistook them
For something else –
Stories, that
Wrote themselves.

Now they arrive
Slowly,
From far away
Waking me from sleep
Draped
In human form
Rapping
Tapping,
At my chamber door.
Masquerading
As dream
They waken me
Tapping at me
Rapping at me as
I try to catch them
To find out what they want,
But they have
No meaning.

Mit Senoj, at the Manchester Contemporary

Mit likes
Simplicity
And colour.
His thoughts
Pop up
Like he does
At launches,
Rich in invention,
And he paints
Hurriedly
In case
They slip away.

'Woodland Near Otley', Phill Hopkins

Shall I go amongst these marvels again
Walk among these wonders
My curiosity sated
And have no care?

•

Like an old husk
Speeding through the black.
Like a quartz
Prince resting
Going nowhere.

Birds' nests
Float gently down
In the dark sky.
It's the last
Spectacular.

•

Laden arms
Of hawthorn in the
Young sun,
A figure
In red walking
To her car,
The sounds of
Canada Geese
Finding
Their partners.
Rain splashes
On the window

Daydream

I leapt up
Knocked the ball
Climbed up higher
Knocked it again
And pedalled
Like a spaceman

Birthday Poem for M

With meaning swift
And eye so sure
And colours
Brought to shape
By gifted hands
With delicate touch,
Your love breathes
Small miracles
Of light
Upon the world.

Thank you
Darling Pea
For so much beauty –
From one of many
Who have felt the
Pleasure of
Your bounty!

(In 2019 Sara was ordained and took the Buddhist name Moksavadini.)

Publication History

Some of these poems first appeared in:

Necrophiliac (eds. Ric Barman, David William Charlesworth, Andy Mason & Dave Wilson)

Manchester Independent (ed. Anna Ford)

New Worlds (eds. Michael Moorcock and Charles Platt)

Ambit (eds. Martin Bax and JG Ballard)

Quill (ed. Michael Thomas)

Lyric (ed. Rowland Winn)

Breakthru (ed. Ken Geering)

Growth (eds. Dave Robinson & Peter Kirkham)

Curtains (ed. Paul Buck)

Skylight (ed. Peter Baker)

Platform (eds. Andrew & Jim Cozens, Cynthea Corres and Paul Robinson)

Zimri (ed. Lisa I Conesa)

Sepia (ed. CD Webb)

Dodo (Australia, eds. Keith Shadwick & Michael Witts)

Ugly Duckling (eds. Keith Richmond & Susan Jane March)

Meuse (Australia, eds. Les Wicks & Bill Farrow)

Umbral (USA, ed. Steve Rasnic)

Ludd's Mill (eds. Andrew Darlington & Steve Sneyd)

Kudos (ed. Graham Sykes)

Peeping Tom (ed. Cory Harding)

Cipher (eds. Jake Tilson & Stephen Whitaker)

Smile (ed. Andy Martin)

Caption (ed. Jenni Scott & roving ed. Del Rooney)

Emanations (USA, ed. Carter Kaplan)

Speculative Fictions (ed. Gareth Jackson)

Simultaneous Times (USA, ed. Jean-Paul L Garnier)

About the Author

MICHAEL BUTTERWORTH is a UK author, publisher and editor. He was a key part of the UK New Wave of Science Fiction in the 1960s, contributing fiction to *New Worlds* and other publications. In 1975 he founded Savoy Books with David Britton, co-authoring Britton's controversial novel *Lord Horror.* In 2009 he launched the contemporary visual art and writing journal *Corridor8.* His latest works are the eponymously titled *Butterworth* (NULL23, 2019) – a collection of his New Wave-era fiction – and a novel, *My Servant the Wind* (also NULL23), based on his 1971 writing notebooks, which develops themes found in his early writing and *Complete Poems.*

About Jim Burns

JIM BURNS is one of England's longest serving and most prolific commentators on the subjects of jazz, alternative literature and avant-garde culture. He is a widely published essayist and critic; also a magazine editor and poet. His poetry was selected for the generation-defining collection *Children of Albion – Poetry of the Underground in Britain,* edited by Michael Horovitz. He has since published over thirty books and pamphlets, including two 'selected poems' collections.

Burns' work had first appeared in leading small-press magazines in the early sixties before he launched his own Mimeo Revolution magazine *Move,* which featured emergent American poets alongside key figures in the British Poetry Revival. He later edited *Palantir* from 1976 to 1983.

Burns was a regular contributor to the iconic literary journal *Ambit* and has appeared on the BBC and in national publications such as *The Guardian, The New Statesman, Tribune* and *New Society.*